What People Are Saying about *WisdomWalks*...

I've always asked God to surround me with people who inspire me to walk more deeply in my pursuit of Him. In this, He has truly been faithful. I can't say enough about the influence (positive or negative) people have on us. We usually become who we hang out with. Dan and Jimmy get this. **WisdomWalks is a read you should check out.**

> **TobyMac,** Grammy-Award recording artist

Jesus transformed the world through the power of relationships, and so can we. That's why I'm giving *WisdomWalks* to everyone I know, so **we can all leave a legacy that matters.**

> **Jon Gordon**, consultant, author of international best sellers
> *The Energy Bus, Training Camp*

WisdomWalks calls men and women to become passionate about this young generation that is overwhelmed by culture. It provides what it promises—**confidence and courage to meet the needs of those who are desperate for spiritual parents, godly mentors, and powerful leaders.**

> **Becky Tirabassi**, author, speaker, life coach

There is nothing about a walk pitchers enjoy, but *WisdomWalk*s is a great tool for mentoring and transferring truth to a teammate, family member, or friend. It's **a walk even I can recommend!**

> **Andy Pettitte**, Pitcher, World Champion New York Yankees

Read and learn from this book! Apply these principles. **Be that voice for the next generation**, so your children too can be powerful difference makers.

> **Carey Casey**, CEO, National Center for Fathering,
> author of *Championship Fathering*

Mentoring is **how Jesus changed the world.** This engaging, hands-on tool gets you moving in that same direction.

> **MELODY CARLSON**, best-selling author,
> *Diary of a Teenage Girl, TrueColors*

A fresh, relevant way to teach the next generation the power and influence of wisdom. **Encourages a lifelong pursuit of excellence.**

> **DON COLBERT**, M.D., *New York Times* best-selling author,
> *The Seven Pillars of Health, Eat This and Live!*

The writers of this book are the real deal—guys who display Christ and help you love God more. **Experience this exciting spiritual adventure** with a group of friends.

> **RON FORSETH,** Vice President, Outreach, Inc., General Editor,
> SermonCentral.com

A spiritual home run for personal growth, discipleship, and mentoring. Biblical, practical, inspiring, and digestible—I'm all in!

> **CHIP INGRAM**, Senior Pastor, Venture Christian Church,
> President, Living on the Edge ministry

Encourages you to **get wisdom, grow in wisdom, and give wisdom.** To live life to the fullest and impact the world around you.

> **LEAH AMICO**, three-time Olympic Gold Medalist

Whether you're in the locker room, the board room, or the living room, if you're intentional about walking like Jesus, you will influence people. *WisdomWalks* gives you **a winning game plan** to invest biblical truth in the lives of others.

> **MATT STOVER**, twenty-year NFL player (Baltimore Ravens,
> Indianapolis Colts, Cleveland Browns, New York Giants)

Lots of people talk about the importance of engaging the next generation and passing on the faith. Dan Britton and Jimmy Page do it. **Read, embrace, and live this book,** and you'll ensure another faith-filled generation will follow.

> **DAN WEBSTER**, Founder, Authentic Leadership, Inc., formerly on staff with Willow Creek Community Church

A simple, practical way to pass on truth. **A must read for those who desire to help raise up the next generation!**

> **NANCY ALCORN**, Founder and President, Mercy Ministries

Young and old alike search for that understandable difference maker to guide them as they seek to develop their relationship with God. With *WisdomWalks*, **lives will be changed forever!**

> **JIM TRESSEL,** head football coach, Ohio State Buckeyes, former fifteen-year head coach, Youngstown State

A great resource for parents, coaches, and anyone who cares about kids and their futures.

> **LES STECKEL**, President/CEO, Fellowship of Christian Athletes, twenty-two-year NFL coach

With *WisdomWalks'* **heart-impacting stories, timeless truths, and meaningful Scripture**, I can say to young women I mentor, "Listen to this!"

> **TRICIA GOYER,** award-winning author, *Life Interrupted, Songbird under a German Moon*

A prescription for anyone who wants to grow in Christ, written by men who have done just that!

> **KYLE ROTE JR.,** 2010 Soccer Hall of Fame, ESPN's "Greatest All-Round Athlete of All Time," national commentator for CBS, PBS, USA Cable

A powerful collection of incredible insights, practical exercises, and **motivation that will get results in both personal and professional endeavors**. Find a place in your briefcase or on your bedstand for this!

STEVE NEWTON, Regional VP, Outback Steakhouse

For those who know we are called to be salt and light but don't always know how, *WisdomWalks* gives the how in a fresh, practical way.

JAMI SMITH, premiere worship leader, recording artist,
Faith in You (Top Worship Album, 2008), *Verse*

A very **useful, practical field guide** based upon forty biblical principles that get one to "true north." Packed with wisdom and eternal truths.

TOM OSBORNE, Athletic Director, University of Nebraska,
former twenty-five-year head coach of the Huskers, author,
More Than Winning

Equips you **to maximize your relationships into conversations that transfer biblical truths into daily wisdom.**

KEN WHITTEN, Senior Pastor, Idlewild Baptist Church

Dan and Jimmy didn't invent mentoring, just the mentoring game plan. I know these two FCA leaders personally, and **you will be blessed by their powerful insights!**

JAMES B. "BUCK" MCCABE, CFO, Chick-fil-A, Inc.

LIVE INTENTIONALLY.
MAXIMIZE RELATIONSHIPS. PASS THE TORCH.

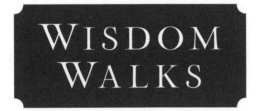

WISDOM
WALKS

40 LIFE PRINCIPLES
for a SIGNIFICANT
& MEANINGFUL
JOURNEY

DAN BRITTON AND JIMMY PAGE

summerside
PRESS™

Summerside Press™
Minneapolis 55438
www.summersidepress.com
WisdomWalks
© 2010 by Dan Britton and Jimmy Page

ISBN 978-1-935416-61-6

Cover and interior design by Chris Gilbert

Author photos © 2010 by Dan Michael Hodges

*Summerside Press™ is an inspirational publisher offering fresh,
irresistible books to uplift the heart and engage the mind.*

Printed in USA

Dedication

To all the WisdomWalkers
who walk with Jesus
and have a passion to invest in others.

To our wives, Dawn and Ivelisse,
who pour heart and soul into the next generation,
investing everything in what really matters.
Without you, there would be no book. You truly make us better men—
better husbands, better fathers, and better friends.

To our kids, our daily reminders to stay on the path:
Kallie, Abigail, and Elijah Britton; Jimmy, Jacob, John, and Grace Page.
You inspire us to follow Jesus and show you the way.
You are our greatest joy.

To our parents:
Dottie and Ed (a man of passion and urgency
who passed to eternity May 2, 2008) Britton
Raymond and Susan Page

And a special thanks to Puchy Ryder, Ivelisse's mom:
a true prayer warrior who stands in the gap!

Acknowledgments

What an incredible journey! Since becoming accountability partners and life friends in 1990, God has surrounded us with a multitude of Wisdom-Walkers who have invested in us, pushed us to be authentic in every area of life, and inspired us to do great things.

Deep appreciation to the All-Star Team at Summerside Press: Carlton, Jason, Joanie, and Ramona. Your enthusiasm for *WisdomWalks* and our shared passion for changing the world inspired us to do our best work, to honor God, and to finish well.

Hats off to Mat Casner for building our online *WisdomWalks* community.

FCA is the most amazing ministry in the world. Special thanks to the entire FCA team: the men and women who walk with Jesus and faithfully invest in the next generation of coaches and athletes. Notable thanks to true servant leaders: Les Steckel, Donnie Dee, Ken Williams, and Tom Rogeberg.

To our friends and family, who've made their mark on us: Scott Steiner, John Patton, Ward Kinne, Tim Fisher, Chris Regan, Sean McNamara, John and Kimarie Page, Tracey Jolley, Lou Santoni, Jon Bisset, Pastor Joe Duke, Tricia Duke, Bryan Kelly, Dale Waters, Joe Knotts, Steve Livernois, Dave Britton, Steve Britton, Barry Spofford, Chris Anderson, Legacy Christian Church, LifePoint Church, all our Community Group Families, 95.1 SHINE FM. To all those we didn't have enough room to mention, we thank you.

To our heavenly Father, for giving us Jesus,
the ultimate WisdomWalker, to show us the way,
the truth, and the life.

TABLE OF CONTENTS

SMART TALKS, WISE WALKS

He who walks with the wise grows wise.

PROVERBS 13:20

I have to hand it to wise ol' King Solomon. He certainly made his share of mistakes during his lifetime (hmm, sounds like somebody else I know), but he also came up with a wealth of wisdom that has influenced my choices—and countless others'—over the generations.

Who doesn't want to be smarter about which life paths to choose? About everyday decisions? About which friends to make—and keep?

And who doesn't want to make a difference in the world? To leave some imprint on humankind that says, "The world is a better place because I've been in it"?

Of all the people who've made an imprint on the world, Jesus Christ is, hands down, the one Person who turned the world upside down. That's because He not only *talked* wisdom, He *walked* in wisdom and *lived out* wisdom. Day by day, in every relational connection, He told stories, asked questions, and referred people back to God's words.

WisdomWalks is modeled after the way Jesus walked, talked, and lived. It isn't a devotional or a program. It's an *experience* that provides the perfect opportunity to grow yourself—and to grow others who accompany you on your life journey. The real-life, relatable stories are intriguing, the life principles stick with you throughout the day, and the provoking questions and Scripture study prompt you to think more deeply about forty key areas of life where decisions you make every moment not only matter, but matter greatly: integrity, friendship, prayer, forgiveness, and faith, to name a few. After all, it's the tough choices you make all along the way that end up being the most significant decisions for your future.

WisdomWalks is a compact game plan by two highly respected Fellowship of Christian Athletes (FCA) national leaders who not only talk the walk, but walk the talk. They're serious about the business of seeing lives change—yours, your loved ones', your coworkers', your neighbors', and whoever else might be in your sphere of influence—because they believe that *you can make a difference*. And so do I. I've spent a lifetime marveling over the incredible impact *one person* can have on the world. Why not you?

So do it for yourself. Carve these forty key life principles into your heart and mind. Allow the truths of God's Word to seep into everything you do. Follow after Jesus, the ultimate WisdomWalker, every moment of the day. Become a WisdomWalker yourself—someone who intentionally pursues and creates spiritual, life-changing connections.

And then make your life contagious! Make a difference in people's lives. Be a joy-spreader. Be a faith-spreader. Be intentional about doing life together with others. Go out of your way to meet people, talk with them, and get to know them. There's nothing I believe in more than passing on core values, faith, and practical life lessons to the next generation. It's what my life's work has been all about.

That's why I think of *WisdomWalks* as Smart Talks, Wise Walks. When you know what to do and you're smart enough to do it (and I know you are), you'll walk with the wise and become wise.

WisdomWalks will transform the way you think—the way you do life. And you'll be a better person for it.

Guaranteed.

DR. KEVIN LEMAN

Internationally known psychologist, humorist, and *New York Times* bestselling author of nearly 40 books about marriage and family issues, including *Have a New Kid by Friday*, *The Birth Order Book*, Dr. Kevin Leman has taught and entertained audiences worldwide with his wit and commonsense psychology, making thousands of house calls for *Fox & Friends*, *The View*, *Fox's The Morning Show*, *Today*, *Oprah*, CBS's *The Early Show*, *Janet Parshall's America* and *Talking It Over, Live! with Regis and Kelly*, CNN's *American Morning*, *Life Today* with James Robison, and *Good Morning America*.

WISDOMWALKS
TO LIVE AND GIVE

It's time to engage.
Make your life count.

In the movie *The Incredibles* Bob and Helen Parr are raising three kids who have superpowers. One night the older two are fighting, Bob is in the other room, completely worn-out and detached, and Helen yells at the top of her lungs, while holding off the sparring siblings, "Bob, it's time to engage! Do something! Don't just stand there! I need you to intervene!"

It's all too easy to gravitate toward "shutdown mode" when life gets crazy. But life never slows down; it gets more hectic and complicated every day. In the midst of this busyness, we lose our ability to live purposefully. It's like we're constantly playing defense, reacting to life instead of creating meaning in it. So instead of doing something, we unplug. We sit on the sidelines and watch life happen.

Disengaging isn't the answer—not for us, and not for those counting on us. Guess who the next generation is looking to for wisdom? You and me. We can play a significant role in their lives, helping them become all that God wants them to be. We can pass on to them a game plan that prepares them for challenges and opportunities and reveals to them God's truth in a relevant, practical way.

Living intentionally, maximizing relationships, and passing the torch of faith was the example Jesus set when He poured His truth and wisdom into His disciples. It's a desire God set in each of our hearts: to transfer our beliefs to others. But it won't happen automatically. You have to be intentional.

WisdomWalks is all about sharing your experiences of God's presence and personal connection. It's about stepping up to the plate and doing what God has called you to do. In Psalm 145:4, David declared, "One generation will declare Your works to the next and will proclaim Your mighty acts" (HCSB). But most of us don't know how to do that. We desire to make an impact on those around us, but often we don't act because: (1) we don't know how to engage in that kind of relationship, (2) we don't feel qualified to do so, and (3) busy schedules get in the way.

For twenty years, the two of us have been WisdomWalking together. Funny thing is, we didn't even know it—at least we didn't call it that in the beginning. The two of us linked arms to do life instead of trying to handle it on our own. As a result, we've both had opportunities to *get* wisdom, to *grow* in wisdom, and to *give* wisdom. And we've passed the blessing on— intentionally and successfully pouring lessons of faith into our children and a host of other individuals we've mentored over the years.

WisdomWalks is designed for multiple uses: for individuals, for study/ discussion groups, and for mentoring relationships. Each WisdomWalk comes from a real-life experience and is a reminder to walk like Jesus, talk like Jesus, and live like Jesus. Jesus used images of bread, water, meals, and money to show us who He is and how we are called to live. WisdomWalks are modern-day parables that reveal forty of the most important life principles you can live out and give to others.

Each WisdomWalk has a specific order to guide you through each experience. There are three basic sections:

WisdomWalk Principle

- Introduces the key life principle and shares a true-to-life *WisdomWalks* story.

WisdomWalking

- Connects the truth of Scripture with the *WisdomWalks* Principle and includes "Be a WisdomWalker!" questions to kick off individual reflection and/or group discussion.

A Step Deeper

- Encourages you to *Live It* through individual action, *Maximize It* through connection with a friend, mentor, or mentoree, and *Pass It On* by studying and sharing additional Bible passages. You can

Foothill Section Ministers
Christmas Dinner & Meeting
Thursday, Dec 1, 2011 6:30 PM

Dinner will be served

RSVP Mandatory 916-652-6884 or to
loomisaog@sbcglobal.net
(put Christmas dinner in subject line)

Please bring a gift for exchange ($10 limit)
Dress - Christmas Attire

First Assembly of God
6217 Brace Rd
Loomis, CA 95650

Bethel Church

13010 State Hwy 49

Grass Valley, CA 95949

Morrice L Cunningham
5775 King Rd
Loomis, CA 95650-8779

journal your "aha moments" along the way in *My Insights*. Each WisdomWalk ends with a prayer of commitment and connection.

WisdomWalks work—they energize and transform lives. We know, because they've done just that to *our* lives, and the lives of every person we've used them with over the years! When you live intentionally, maximize your relationships, and pass the torch, you become passionate about life, excited about relationships, and your desire to understand and know God is ramped up. Every moment becomes an adventure because you wonder, *What is God going to do next? And how can I intentionally be a part of that?*

WisdomWalks Is Not a Formula; It's a *Field Manual*

This is not about A + B = C. You don't have to be a Bible scholar to qualify. You don't have to have all the answers. This is not a formula for success. It's a practical, in-the-trenches guide to help you pour life-changing principles and practices into your own and others' hearts and minds as you grow in faith and navigate your unique circumstances.

WisdomWalks Is Not a Result; It's a *Relationship*

This is not about achieving a goal. It's not something you check off your "to-do" list. Instead, it's about relationships. It's about intentionally investing your life in getting to know God more, and then intentionally investing in the lives of others to build a godly foundation and grow their desire for an intimate relationship with Jesus Christ.

WisdomWalks Is Not a Moment; It's a *Movement*

This is not about crossing a finish line or driving a stake in the ground. It's not the latest fad or a resolution to live better that you'll forget within a month or two. It is part of a lifelong movement to walk as Jesus did, to follow in His steps, and to encourage others to walk with Him.

God has planted seeds of greatness—our very own "superpowers"— in each of us. And He'll use us to cultivate those seeds in others—but only if we will engage. So what are you waiting for? Make your life count!

DAN BRITTON AND JIMMY PAGE

Walking in wisdom has no finish line.
It's a lifelong pursuit.

JIMMY PAGE

Whoever claims to live in him
must walk as Jesus did.

1 JOHN 2:6

A WALK WITH THE WISE

WisdomWalks Principle
Friends will make you or break you.

*We need people who influence their peers
and who cannot be detoured from their convictions.*

JOE PATERNO

Bear Grylls, star of the TV show *Man vs. Wild,* is no stranger to danger. From the time he was a little boy, he always dreamed of climbing Mount Everest—one of the world's most difficult, dangerous mountains. Bear's determination won out. At twenty-three, he became the youngest Briton ever to reach the summit.

On the mountain, extreme weather changes, lack of oxygen, and risk of avalanche make death a present danger for even the most experienced mountaineers. Bear would have died himself if it weren't for his skillful teammate, who literally held Bear's life in his hands as he dangled unconsciously from a single rope.

Making the ascent to the summit without the help of the Sherpas, or experienced, skillful guides, is virtually impossible. Climbers learn to trust their guide completely. They attach themselves to ropes expertly anchored by the Sherpas, who have gone before them. They follow the exact path marked out for them and pay attention to warnings.

In life, how well we navigate is also dependent in large part on the quality and character of our friends. The friends we choose, our trusted inner circle, can make or break us. And we can make or break them.

Back when I was a kid, my parents always told me, "Choose your friends wisely." In fact, they would ask me who I was going to be with before they gave their okay. Now I do the same thing with my kids. The influence of peers is profound—for better and for worse. And trusted friendships become even more significant as we grow older.

He who walks with the wise grows wise,
but a companion of fools suffers harm....
A man of many companions may come to ruin,
but there is a friend who sticks closer than a brother.

PROVERBS 13:20; 18:24

The book of Proverbs is all about wisdom—or skillful living. It talks over and over again about the importance of choosing the right friends. Who we spend our time with will either make us more skilled at living or lead us into trouble. Bad company corrupts good morals (1 Corinthians 15:33). It's amazing how clear and simple it is:

Walk with wise friends = get wiser.
Follow foolish friends = get into trouble.

Three great principles in these passages will help you be wise and walk with the wise:

1. *Be a good friend.* To attract faithful friends, you have to become the type of friend you want to be around. If you are trustworthy and honest, you'll be attracted to people who are trustworthy and honest. If you want friends who share your faith and are growing in their relationship with Christ, you'll need to focus on growing spiritually as well. If you don't want friends who gossip, then don't gossip. If you want friends to support you when life is tough, then be loyal, believe the best in them, and defend them when others are tearing them down. If you want friends who do the right things, then you do the right things. Treat others the way God wants you to treat them.

2. *Spend time with friends who are wise.* It doesn't take long to figure out if a friend is wise. Just ask yourself these four simple questions:

   a. Do they follow Jesus, and are they growing in His ways?
   b. Do they do the right thing even when it's hard?
   c. Do they make other people around them better?
   d. Do they stay close when times are tough?

3. *Don't have too many friends.* That sounds a bit odd, doesn't it? Can you ever have too many friends? After all, isn't life all about relationships? The answer is both yes and no. The key is to have an inner circle of close friends that you have developed trust with over time. These are your go-to people—the ones you can count on to be honest with you no matter what. Even Jesus, within his group of twelve, had an inner circle of just three—Peter, James, and John—with whom He had a deeper level of trust and closeness. When you let too many in to that inner circle, it can devalue the most important friendships you have.

Wise friends help us navigate life successfully. Being a wise friend brings life to others as well.

Be a WisdomWalker!

How are you doing as a friend? Give yourself a letter grade for each of the questions below, and explain why you rated yourself that way. Do you:

- follow Jesus? Are you growing in His ways?

- do the right thing even when it's hard?

- make other people around you better?

- stay close when times are tough for your friends?

What two specific things could you change to become a better friend?

A Step Deeper

Live Intentionally. Maximize Your Relationships. Pass the Torch.

Live It

1. Spend some time with God in prayer.
2. Ask God to reveal where you need to improve as a friend.
3. Write down everything He tells you in the "My Insights" section.

4. Confess any wrongdoing and sinful behavior and ask Him to forgive you.
5. Ask Him to give you the courage and determination to change what needs to be changed.

Maximize It

1. Write down the names of your closest friends. Take a careful look at each one. Are they wise—or foolish? Are they following Jesus, doing the right things, making you better, and are they loyal in tough times?
2. Which two or three people in your life might fit the qualities of a good friend? People you'd like to become better friends with? Brainstorm how to connect with those people in a more meaningful way.

Pass It On

For additional study, read and reflect on:

- Proverbs 14:12
- 1 Corinthians 15:33
- 2 Corinthians 6:14–18

Share one of the above Scriptures with a friend or family member—and talk about how its wisdom and truth has influenced you to make some changes in your life.

My Insights

_____

_____

_____

_____

Father, I know good friendships are so important. Help me to be a trustworthy, loyal friend—to make others around me better and to do the right things, even when it's hard. Lead me to an inner circle of friends who love You and walk in wisdom. May we challenge each other to become everything You designed us to be.

2

WALKIE-TALKIE

WisdomWalks Principle
Be the person you want others to become.

God's dream is that Christians
would actually live like Christians.

CHIP INGRAM

When my two older brothers and I were kids, we invented a game called Walkie-Talkie. I'm pretty sure now it was just a game that allowed my brothers to inflict bodily harm on me, but I wasn't smart enough then to figure that out. I was merely thankful they wanted to do something with their youngest brother.

I know a walkie-talkie is a portable, handheld communication device, but we hijacked the name because it perfectly fit our game. We would walk side by side through the house with our arms over each other's shoulders and say out loud, "Walkie-Talkie," with each step. The way to win the game was by suddenly trying to trip the other person by throwing them to the ground. One time my brother won when I flew face-first into my mom's showcase furniture. Thirty-three years later, there's still clear evidence that my front tooth took out a chunk of wood and found a new home.

Recently I was thinking about that game while reflecting on my spiritual walk. Sometimes it feels like I'm playing *spiritual* Walkie-Talkie. Over the years, I've walked shoulder-to-shoulder with people (coworkers, teammates, family, friends) who have later tried to "take me out" because a competitive spirit developed. Just as my brothers and I wanted to win the game at all costs, each of us has a desire to be victorious. We want to outperform others or be one step ahead. And sometimes we not only want to win in life, we want to defeat others.

I confess: I quickly get sucked into this game of Walkie-Talkie. It's at those times when I need a good friend to walk with me side-by-side—someone who sees how I live, gets to know me well, and is trustworthy to hold me accountable when I need it.

WisdomWalking

I urge you to imitate me.

1 CORINTHIANS 4:16

I always thought this statement of the apostle Paul's was rather arrogant—after all, he's telling people they should imitate him—until I realized what Paul was really saying. What a statement of accountability! It would have been far easier for him to say, "Okay, folks, I urge you to imitate Jesus Himself." But instead, Paul was willing to put his own walk with Christ in the spotlight. He wanted others to examine his life for authenticity. He wanted others to see that he was so close to Jesus, so intimate with and in love with Him, that everything in his life backed up that statement. Paul was saying, "Hey, if you want to walk with me for a couple hours, you'll get a full understanding of what the life of Christ was all about."

When others walk with you, what do they see? Is your faith in Christ real and authentic? Are you the real deal? In 1 Corinthians 4:20, Paul says the kingdom of God isn't just a lot of talk; it's living by God's power—and our lives should be evidence of His power. When others rub shoulders with you, do they see a life filled with hope, love, joy, peace, and humility? Do they come face-to-face with a walking, talking example of Jesus living in and through you?

Our world is dying to see what a fully surrendered Christian looks like. Man, count me in! I want people to walk with me and find out I'm the real deal. I want to become more like Christ every day so His light and love shine through to others. Now *that's* the game of Walkie-Talkie I want to play for the rest of my life. How about you?

Be a WisdomWalker!

How do you respond to Paul's statement, "So I urge you to imitate me"? Does it scare you? Motivate you? Intimidate you? Explain.

Is your walk stronger than your talk? Why or why not? What would it take for your talk and walk to line up?

A Step Deeper

Live Intentionally. Maximize Your Relationships. Pass the Torch.

Live It

1. Spend some time with God in prayer.
2. Ask God to reveal to you the differences between your walk and your talk.
3. Write down everything He tells you in the "My Insights" section.
4. Confess any wrongdoing and sinful behavior and ask Him to forgive you.
5. Ask Him to give you the courage and determination to change what needs to be changed.

Maximize It

1. Ask a trusted friend or family member if he/she sees Jesus in you—and, if so, what qualities or traits he/she can identify.
2. How might you be able to more fully show, through your life and actions, who Jesus is?

3. Think of someone who brings you close to Christ every time you are around him/her. What is it about that person's life that makes you respond that way? In what way(s) could you emulate those same character traits and/or life experiences?

Pass It On

For additional study, read and reflect on:

- 1 Corinthians 4:14–17
- Ephesians 5:1–2
- Hebrews 6:12; 13:7

Share one of the above Scriptures with a friend or family member— and talk about how its wisdom and truth has influenced you to make some changes in your life.

My Insights

_____

_____

_____

_____

_____

_____

_____

Lord, I want my life so consumed by Your love that others see and feel the difference. When people get close to me and know my heart, I pray they will see the real deal. Help me to be authentic about my faith—to live in such a way that my everyday actions and lifestyle attract others to You. May my walk be worthy of the Gospel. In the name of Jesus Christ I pray. Amen.

3

GIGO

WisdomWalks Principle
What's in the well comes up in the bucket.

Sow a thought, reap an action.
Sow an action, reap a habit.
Sow a habit, reap a character.
Sow a character, reap a destiny.

RANDY ALCORN

When I was in college, my computer teacher introduced me to the acronym GIGO. It stands for "Garbage In—Garbage Out." She stressed to us students the importance of not filling our computer's storage with corrupt files. After all, what we put into the computer would eventually come out (or, as I discovered too many times to count, bad files would cause my computer to crash).

As an athlete, I got the same talk from my lacrosse coaches. "If you fill your body with junk, that's exactly what will come out. Junk. A poor performance on the field. Got it?" I got it, especially since I had heard basically the same litany from my mom as I was growing up: "If you eat junk food, that's how you're going to feel—like junk. What you put into your body will make all the difference in what you get out of it."

Good ol' Mom. She was right then, and her words are still right on now. I always feel better when I'm eating healthy foods, taking care of myself, and getting the sleep and regroup time I need to feel 100 percent.

But the concept of GIGO is even more powerful and life-changing when you apply it to your heart. What's in your heart's well will always come up in the bucket.

Guard your heart above all else, for it is the source of life.

PROVERBS 4:23 HCSB

I love this wise saying from the book of Proverbs, because it reminds me to guard my heart from the garbage that otherwise can make its way in. If you squeeze a tube of toothpaste, what comes out? Mustard? No, toothpaste, because that's what was put in the tube. That means if you put garbage in your heart—jealousy, lying, degrading images, anger, competitiveness, etc.—that's exactly what will come out. And just as garbage in real life can get stinky, so can your attitudes and actions.

I like to think about G.I.G.O. not as Garbage In, Garbage Out but rather as God In, God Out. If you are putting God into our heart every day, thinking of Him, studying His Word, talking about Him with others, then God will come out.

The real test comes when you're under pressure. When you're getting the squeeze, what's coming out of your life—God, or garbage? The answer to that question will have everything to do with how you interact with God and with others, and how you feel about yourself and the events of each day.

Be a WisdomWalker!

The last time you were squeezed, what came out? God—or garbage? Explain, using a real-life example.

What specific garbage do you let enter your heart? Why? What can you do the next time you have the choice of whether to allow the garbage in or God in?

A Step Deeper

Live Intentionally. Maximize Your Relationships. Pass the Torch.

Live It

1. Spend some time with God in prayer.
2. Ask God to reveal to you any garbage you allow into your heart.
3. Write down everything He tells you in the "My Insights" section.
4. Confess any wrongdoing and sinful behavior and ask Him to forgive you.
5. Ask Him to give you the courage and determination to change what needs to be changed.

Maximize It

1. Discuss with a trusted friend how garbage gets into your heart. When does it happen? Where does it happen? How does it happen? Identify the specifics.
2. Talk about ways in which you can guard against that particular form of garbage getting into your heart.
3. Brainstorm some steps you can take today to ensure that you focus on getting God In, and God Out.

Pass It On

For additional study, read and reflect on:

- Luke 11:39
- James 1:2–4

Share one of the above Scriptures with a friend or family member—and talk about how its wisdom and truth has influenced you to make some changes in your life.

My Insights

_____

_____

_____

_____

_____

_____

_____

_____

_____

_____

Lord, I know my heart is the wellspring of life. I desire to walk in Your truth, keeping my heart pure. Guard my heart from garbage that can creep in, and keep my mind alert to its presence if it is there already. When the pressure comes, help me to stand firm and to focus on You, and You alone.

4

GAP-FREE LIVING

WisdomWalks Principle
What you see is what you get.

People with integrity have nothing to hide and nothing to fear.
Their lives are open books.
WARREN W. WIERSBE

A favorite story of mine is a legendary tale that occurred during one of the most intense times of the French Revolution.

A man is seen running after a mob—and straight into danger.

"Stop!" another man calls after him. "Stop! Don't follow that mob!"

But the first man continues to sprint toward the mob, and as he runs, he calls back to the other man, "But I have to follow them! I'm their leader!"

When I first heard Bible teacher Warren W. Wiersbe tell that story, I laughed. It truly is funny when things don't appear to be the way they actually are. But then I sobered when I contemplated the serious side of the story. How often does this happen to us spiritually? How often do we live completely differently than the image we try to convey to others?

As a professional lacrosse player, I knew some of my teammates were big partiers. But here's the kicker: they lived with more integrity than I did! As a Christian who had a "testimony" to protect, I tried to hide my gaps. What they said and did, however, were the same things. No gaps. Just the basic "what you see is what you get" lifestyle—straight-up truth. No hypocrisy there.

It made me wonder. What would my life look like if who I was on the inside and who I was on the outside lined up? If there was no gap between my beliefs and my behavior?

What would *your* life look like?

The integrity of the upright guides them,
but the unfaithful are destroyed by their duplicity.

PROVERBS 11:3

Legendary UCLA basketball coach John Wooden once said, "A leader's most powerful ally is his or her own example. There is hypocrisy to the phrase, 'Do as I say, not as I do.' I refused to make demands on my boys that I wasn't willing to live out in my own life."

The *duplicity* this verse in Proverbs is talking about is just a big word for *gaps.* Gaps happen when honesty and truth—the two key ingredients of integrity—become options instead of non-negotiable standards. And the gap between who you are on the outside and who you are on the inside can lead to great tension. Living with gaps won't bring life-change; it'll bring inner torment. Proverbs says it will even destroy you.

You see, there's a constant war in our souls. We don't want others to see us as we really are because they might see that we are imperfect. But God wants us to bring the dark things—those hidden things we've buried deep within our hearts—into the light so that He can purify us.

When who you are on the outside matches who you are on the inside, you have wholeness, completeness, soundness. You are the same throughout, and you are living in honesty and truth.

God doesn't want gaps in your life. He wants every corner of your life to be so filled with honesty and truth that there are no gaps between your beliefs and your behavior. When you're authentic—not perfect, but real—your life will change, and others' lives will change. Families, schools, communities, even nations will change.

Gap-free living requires guts—spiritual grit and courage. You have to take a stand. No more duplicity. No more pretending. No more hiding. But the results are worth it.

Be a WisdomWalker!

What gaps do you see in your life between who others think you are and who you really are? Be specific.

Why do you think those gaps are there? What in your background and experiences has led to those gaps?

A Step Deeper

Live Intentionally. Maximize Your Relationships. Pass the Torch.

Live It

1. Spend some time with God in prayer.
2. Ask God to reveal to you any gaps that you may have—both those you know about and ones that you aren't yet aware of.
3. Write down everything He tells you in the "My Insights" section.
4. Confess any wrongdoing and sinful behavior and ask Him to forgive you.
5. Ask Him to give you the courage and determination to change what needs to be changed.

Maximize It

1. Talk with a trusted friend about the gaps you've identified in your life—and why you think they're there.
2. Discuss what it means to have spiritual courage. What would that look like in your life?
3. Pray together that God will expose any hidden gaps so you can live in honesty and truth.

Pass It On

For additional study, read and reflect on:

- Galatians 1:10
- Ephesians 3:16–19
- Philippians 3:8–10

Share one of the above Scriptures with a friend or family member—and talk about how its wisdom and truth has influenced you to make some changes in your life.

My Insights

_____

_____

_____

_____

_____

_____

_____

_____

_____

Father, thank You for Your unconditional love for me and for Your desire for me to live a life of honesty and truth. I long to live gap-free—to let Your grace and mercy fill my gaps so there is no room for any duplicity. Jesus, let me fall into Your love and experience a fresh touch from You. Forgive me, Lord, for when I have failed in this area. I ask for spiritual courage today—and every day. Thank You, Lord. In the name of Jesus I pray. Amen.

5

PERMANENT MARKER

WisdomWalks Principle
Leave the mark of Jesus.

*Our days are numbered. One of the primary goals
should be to prepare for our last day.
The legacy we leave is not just in our possessions,
but in the quality of our lives.*

BILLY GRAHAM

I was eight years old when I had a once-in-a-lifetime opportunity to ride my older brother's motorcycle. I wanted to show him how "big" I was, so I took off with reckless abandonment. Then, a hundred yards down the dirt road of my ride to glory, something happened.

My front tire hit a pothole that I never saw. Suddenly, I was airborne... and my life was passing before my eyes.

I landed in a ditch, and the revved-up motorcycle landed on my back!

Thankfully, as a result of being in the ditch, the only part of the motorcycle that touched my back was the muffler. But as the muffler burned through my shirt and my flesh, I experienced a world of hurt. It seemed years, rather than minutes, before my brother rescued me.

I was banned from riding his bike ever again.

Even though that event happened many years ago, to this day you can see a burn imprint on my back. That muffler left its mark!

Each of us also leave an imprint behind in life. In everything we do and say, we leave a mark on others. Will it be a good impression or a bad impression? That's up to you.

But there's even more to consider.

I have been crucified with Christ; and I no longer live, but Christ lives in me. The life I now live in the flesh, I live by faith in the Son of God, who loved me and gave Himself for me.

GALATIANS 2:19–20 HCSB

For me, the ultimate question is not whether I will leave a good or bad imprint on others. Rather, it's, "Will I leave an imprint of myself—or Jesus?" That's what matters in the long run, doesn't it?

Will others get more of you—or will they get more of Jesus?

Paul wrote in Galatians 2:20 that we need to die to self so that we no longer live. That means no longer thinking of ourselves first, but of others first. No longer thinking what we want to do, but what Christ wants us to do. What a challenge!

But the reward is great: for Christ to live *in* us, and *through* us. That means when you touch others' lives, there's no mark of you. Instead, there's the mark of Christ! Everything you say and do has the potential to leave a mark on others. So regularly ask yourself a series of questions:

1. Were my words encouraging and uplifting? Did I speak truth and life into others?
2. Were my attitudes positive and patient? Did I act with humility and grace?
3. Were my actions appropriate? Did I do the right thing even when it was hard?

These questions always remind me to take a close look at whose mark I may be leaving, and they help remind me to show others a living picture of Jesus.

No matter what you do, be committed to leave behind a lasting imprint—the imprint of Christ.

Be a WisdomWalker!

Think through your interactions with others in the last twenty-four hours. With whom have you interacted? What kind of marks have you left?

Is there anything you wish you had done differently? If so, what?

A Step Deeper

Live Intentionally. Maximize Your Relationships. Pass the Torch.

Live It

1. Spend some time with God in prayer.
2. Ask God to reveal to you the truth about the imprint you're leaving on others.
3. Write down everything He tells you in the "My Insights" section.
4. Confess any wrongdoing and sinful behavior and ask Him to forgive you.
5. Ask Him to give you the courage and determination to change what needs to be changed.

Maximize It

1. Ask a trusted friend or family member, "What kind of imprints do you see me leaving behind?" Listen closely not only for their words, but their feelings.
2. Brainstorm with that friend to find some practical things you could do to make sure the imprint will be God's—and not yours.

Pass It On

For additional study, read and reflect on:

- Psalm 96:7–8
- Romans 14:7–8
- Colossians 3:23

Share one of the above Scriptures with a friend or family member—and talk about how its wisdom and truth has influenced you to make some changes in your life.

My Insights

_____

_____

_____

_____

_____

_____

_____

_____

_____

_____

_____

_____

Lord, I want to leave behind Your mark, and not mine. Help me to focus on You—Your characteristics, Your qualities—so that I will make impressions of You. Help me to die to self, so that only You shine through all I do and all I am.

6

TWEET–TWEET

WisdomWalks Principle
Your words are powerful and permanent.

*From listening comes wisdom,
and from speaking, repentance.*
ITALIAN PROVERB

Oops. Have you ever said something that you wish you could take back? I sure have. In fact, there have been times when that little voice of conscience in my head has advised me, *"Don't say it!"* or, *"You're going to regret this…,"* and still I've been unable to hold my tongue. And then the argument escalates—when I could have diffused it with kindness. Or, I've hurt someone I care deeply about with the things I've said. Sometimes I've wished I had a fishing line attached to my words so I could reel them back in!

Words are a powerful thing. Even though we've all heard the old adage, "Sticks and stones may break my bones, but words will never hurt me," it's not true, is it? We've all experienced pain from what others have said to us. Often we can even remember those hurtful, discouraging words decades later.

Today's technology has created a platform to instantly broadcast our every thought or feeling. Texting, email, websites, and social media platforms like Facebook™ and Twitter™ have totally transformed the ways we communicate. Twitter has become so popular that if you're not "tweeting," eyes roll to tell you you're missing out! You can "Tweet" that you're bored and eating ice cream as long as you use 140 characters or less.

But when you start to read some of the stuff that's being tweeted and how it instantly makes its way around the world into the headlines and onto the talk shows, you realize how careful you have to be with your words. These "tweets" can't be taken back. And they're instantly forwarded from one end of the earth to the other.

All these options create a powerful, permanent record. People have lost their jobs for things they've said through e-mail. Others have broken off relationships with a text message. Athletes openly disagree with decisions of their coaches and team owners. And now colleges and employers are looking at applicants' online identities as they consider them for admissions or employment. A little scary, isn't it?

WisdomWalking

If anyone is never at fault in what he says, he is a perfect man, able to keep his whole body in check. When we put bits into the mouths of horses to make them obey us, we can turn the whole animal. Or take ships as an example. Although they are so large and are driven by strong winds, they are steered by a very small rudder wherever the pilot wants to go. Likewise the tongue is a small part of the body, but it makes great boasts. Consider what a great forest is set on fire by a small spark. The tongue also is a fire, a world of evil among the parts of the body. It corrupts the whole person, sets the whole course of his life on fire...no man can tame the tongue. It is a restless evil, full of deadly poison. With the tongue we praise our LORD and Father, and with it we curse men, who have been made in God's likeness. Out of the same mouth come praise and cursing. My brothers, this should not be.

JAMES 3:2–10

Just as a small bit in the mouth of a horse controls the direction of the horse and a small rudder on a ship controls the direction of the ship, our words—spoken and written—control the direction of our life. They linger on as a permanent record. But if the bit, the rudder, and our tongue are controlled? Each can be used for wonderful purposes. When the horse is under control, it can plow a field. When the ship is controlled, it can deliver great cargo. When the tongue is controlled, we bring life to those around us—through encouragement, praise, compassion, love, and kindness.

The words we speak are an overflow of what's in our heart. Will your words be encouraging or discouraging? Criticism or praise? Life or death? All reflect the state of your heart. The same mouth shouldn't praise God...

and put down others. Or speak Bible verses...and gossip about friends. Words are powerful and permanent. How are you mastering yours?

Be a WisdomWalker!

What one positive thing do you remember a parent, friend, teacher, coach, or other mentor saying to you when you were young? Why do you think you still remember it?

What one negative thing do you remember a parent, friend, teacher, coach, or other mentor saying to you when you were young? How did this comment affect you then? How does it affect you now?

A Step Deeper

Live Intentionally. Maximize Your Relationships. Pass the Torch.

Live It

1. Spend some time with God in prayer.
2. Ask God to reveal to you the truth about the words you speak. Do they reflect what's truly in your heart?
3. Write down everything He tells you in the "My Insights" section.
4. Confess any wrongdoing and sinful behavior and ask Him to forgive you.
5. Ask Him to give you the courage and determination to change what needs to be changed.

Maximize It

1. What is one thing you've said that you wish you could take back? Why?

2. What plan could you put in place to reconcile (if possible) the relationship you damaged? How might you avoid the same situation with someone else?
3. Brainstorm ideas to help you actively remember to think first before you speak or act.

Pass It On
For additional study, read and reflect on:

- Proverbs 10:11, 19; 12:18; 13:3; 15:4; 18:21
- Matthew 15:18
- James 1:19

Share one of the above Scriptures with a friend or family member—and talk about how its wisdom and truth has influenced you to make some changes in your life.

My Insights

_____

_____

_____

_____

_____

_____

Father, help me to be quick to listen, slow to speak, and slow to become angry. Reveal to me the condition of my heart—any envy, anger, or pride—because I know the words that come out of my mouth are a reflection of what's inside me. Help me to be more careful with my tongue, so that my life heads in the direction You've designed it to go. Control my words so I can speak words of life that build up, encourage, and inspire my friends and family.

7

BLIND SPOTS

WisdomWalks Principle
A little humility goes a long way.

There is one way to find out if a man is honest—
ask him. If he says "yes," you know he is crooked.

GROUCHO MARX

One of my favorite TV shows over the years has been *American Idol*. If you're familiar with the program, you know that each season begins with a massive talent search. The show travels to several major cities across the country and invites "regular" Americans to audition—to display their "undiscovered ability" to sing. In each city, tens of thousands of wannabe stars show up and wait in enormously long lines, all for their one big shot to sing in front of Randy, Paula, and Simon, and to fulfill their dream—to become the next *American Idol*.

Anyone who has seen the show knows that the initial auditions are, in general, painful. While some of the auditions are amazing, the vast majority shown on TV are absolutely awful. The person might forget the words, make unearthly screeching noises, sing off-key, and/or wear hideous outfits.

It's not the lack of talent that bothers me. Not really. In fact, that often makes for a very interesting show. What's troublesome is that every single person genuinely believes he can sing with the best of the best. He just hasn't gotten his big break yet! And the worst singers, when asked by the judges why they think they can sing, often say, "Well, all my friends tell me how great I sing." (Just watch the judges' eye-rolls at that overused statement.)

American Idol is a great picture of what's commonly referred to as a "Blind Spot." We all have them—things that we can't see about ourselves that frustrate, annoy, hurt, or anger others. Flaws in our perception about who we really are that prevent us from seeing (or admitting) the truth.

Often, like the *American Idol* contestants, we can't see that we're out of tune…that we have gaps in our attitude or perception or character that God wants to change.

WisdomWalking

To some who were confident of their own righteousness and looked down on everybody else, Jesus told this parable: "Two men went up to the temple to pray, one a Pharisee and the other a tax collector. The Pharisee stood up and prayed about himself: 'God, I thank you that I am not like other men—robbers, evildoers, adulterers—or even like this tax collector. I fast twice a week and give a tenth of all I get.' But the tax collector stood at a distance. He would not even look up to heaven, but beat his breast and said, 'God, have mercy on me, a sinner.' I tell you that this man, rather than the other, went home justified before God. For everyone who exalts himself will be humbled, and he who humbles himself will be exalted."

LUKE 18:9–14

I'd say the Pharisee in the parable has huge blind spots, wouldn't you? I mean, to literally thank God that he isn't like these other evil people—are you serious? Talk about being full of yourself! The Pharisee couldn't wait to pray about himself so he could show off how good he was. That way others could see it too (frankly, how could they miss it?) and praise him for his goodness. The Pharisee did religious stuff—following all the rules for being a "good person"—but couldn't see that his heart was self-centered, prideful, and far from God. No wonder he left the synagogue unchanged.

The tax-collector, on the other hand, was honest about his condition. He was humble. He was honest about his sinful condition and that he needed the great mercy of God in order to be forgiven and changed. He was willing to let God expose his attitudes and his actions so he could come clean. He probably also had friends he could trust who spoke truth to him in a loving way. Friends who could help him see his blind spots. And in his humility before God, he left that synagogue forgiven and free— a *changed* person from the inside out.

We all have blind spots. I do, and you probably do too. But if we get on our knees and humbly ask God to bring them to light, it's amazing what can change in our life and relationships.

As you humble yourself, God will start to lift you up.

Be a WisdomWalker!

In what way(s) can you identify personally with either the Pharisee or the tax collector in the story—or both?

What blind spot(s) might you have? What clues do you see in your life and relationships that might make you think that?

A Step Deeper

Live Intentionally. Maximize Your Relationships. Pass the Torch.

Live It

1. Spend some time with God in prayer.
2. Ask God to reveal to you any blind spots that you may have.
3. Write down everything He tells you in the "My Insights" section.
4. Confess any wrongdoing and sinful behavior and ask Him to forgive you.
5. Ask Him to give you the courage and determination to change what needs to be changed.

Maximize It

1. Ask a trusted friend to be honest with you about any blind spots they see: attitudes you have (anger, selfishness), things you do or don't do, relationships you have, the way you handle money, etc. Getting their insight and perspective is a great way to get a handle on your blind spots.

2. Remember: True friends will tell you what you *need to hear*, not just what you *want to hear*. So take good notes and ask questions so you'll walk away with a full understanding of things you need to change about yourself.
3. Ask God to help you change what needs to be changed—even when it's difficult to change.

Pass It On

For additional study, read and reflect on:

- Mark 2:14–17
- Luke 6:42
- Romans 12:3
- 1 Peter 5:5

Share one of the above Scriptures with a friend or family member—and talk about how its wisdom and truth has influenced you to make some changes in your life.

My Insights

_____

_____

_____

_____

_____

_____

_____

Father, I know that I have blind spots. In Your wisdom, please reveal them to me. Show me any wrong attitude, any thoughts that I think, any words that I speak, anything I do that doesn't honor You. Help me to not think too highly of myself, to not be too hard on myself, and to not compare myself with others. Help me to be honest with myself, with others, and with You.

8

THE MONEY MIRROR

WisdomWalks Principle
Put your money where your heart is.

A checkbook is a theological document.
It will tell you who and what you worship.
BILLY GRAHAM

I was stunned, years ago, when a close friend of mine told me he could tell me instantly what I loved, if I just let him take a look at my checkbook. (Today, he'd have to look at my credit cards as well.) What was my friend trying to say? That we always spend money on things important to us. So whatever I spent the most money on was most likely what I loved the most—and what I spent the least on was probably what I didn't value too much. My money was a mirror to my heart.

I got the message. As I looked through my checkbook, I came face to face with some hard truths. I found out I was giving far less than I thought I was to those in need. In fact, I was surprised at how little I was investing in God's work through my local church and ministries around the world. Worse, I was selfish—spending a disproportionate amount on car payments, eating out, and other leisure and recreational activities.

That was the day I learned two truths:

- If you *follow the money,* you'll *find the heart.*
- If you *follow the heart,* you'll *find the money.*

WisdomWalking

Do not store up for yourselves treasures on earth, where moth and rust destroy, and where thieves break in and steal. But store up for

*yourselves treasures in heaven, where moth and rust do not break in
and steal. For where your treasure is, there your heart will be also.*

MATTHEW 6:19-21

What's Jesus saying in Matthew 6? "If I get to know your heart, I'll be able to easily predict what you spend your money on." And the opposite is also true: "If I take a look at what you spend your money on, I will get to know your heart." How you spend your money can reveal your character, just as adversity or stress does. So:

Get your heart right. I'm not crazy about the fact that my spiritual maturity is easily seen in the way I handle money. But it's true. Money is a mirror that reflects not only what's important to me, but also who I think the money belongs to, and even whom I trust. Do I value the things God values? Do I think I "own" my money and things, or am I a steward of what He's given? Do I trust that God will provide as I work, or am I trying to make everything work out on my own power?

The more you connect with God, the more you realize that everything you have comes from Him. Your role is simply to be a responsible steward.

Invest, don't spend. When you spend money, it's gone. But investments? They typically grow over time. Investing in people and their needs can literally change the present and the future. When you invest in God's work, lives can be changed forever. A wise businessman grows his profits so he has more to give back. A wise farmer invests in seed that grows and is harvested to feed the entire community. A wise fisherman teaches others how to fish, so they can feed themselves and their families. A wise steward finds ways to multiply resources and teaches others how to do the same so they all can give generously to those in need. How are you investing your money?

Think long-term, not short-term. I've never bought anything that didn't break down, get used up, or wear out. Everything on this earth will decay. Does this mean you shouldn't buy things you want and enjoy? No. The question is more: Are you investing your money wisely in what really matters? Are people more important than things? Are your "wants" more important than others' needs? Do you respond generously to others' needs? Do you invest in ministries that share the Gospel of Christ?

Jesus told us that whenever we help those in need, we do it for Him (Matthew 25:35–40). He tells us to be a stream—passing our blessings of money and resources on—rather than a lake, which just accumulates more "stuff." Sometimes you have to lead your heart, and sometimes you need to follow it. When I find myself being selfish, I lead my heart by giving more. When opportunities arise to invest in ministries and families in need, I follow my heart. See how it works?

The more you become like Jesus, the more you'll want what He wants.

Be a WisdomWalker!

What do your checkbook and credit card statements say about where you are spending and investing your money? How does this spending reflect what you love?

Does debt prevent you from giving generously? How could you change your spending habits to allow yourself financial margin?

What is your money mirror revealing to you? What would you like to change?

A Step Deeper

Live Intentionally. Maximize Your Relationships. Pass the Torch.

Live It

1. Spend some time with God in prayer.
2. Ask God to reveal the true state of your heart in your money mirror.
3. Write down everything He tells you in the "My Insights" section.
4. Confess any wrongdoing and sinful behavior and ask Him to forgive you.
5. Ask Him to give you the courage and determination to change what needs to be changed.

Maximize It

1. Talk with a trusted friend about these three questions:
    a. What steps can you take to get your heart right?

b. In what could you invest, instead of simply spending?

c. How can you begin thinking long-term, instead of short-term?

2. What one thing could you reprioritize about where you invest money?

3. Ask your friend to hold you accountable for being a wise steward.

Pass It On

For additional study, read and reflect on:

- Deuteronomy 8:16–18
- Psalm 112
- Matthew 25:14–30, 35–36
- 2 Corinthians 9:6–13

Share one of the above Scriptures with a friend or family member—and talk about how its wisdom and truth has influenced you to make some changes in your life.

My Insights

_____

_____

_____

_____

_____

_____

Father, thank You for giving me the money mirror. I know that how I spend my money can be a reflection of what's going on inside me. It can reveal the condition of my heart and even paint a picture of my spiritual maturity. Lord, help me get my heart right so what's important to You becomes important to me. Help me to put my money where Your heart is and to invest it wisely, for eternal impact.

9

RUMBLE STRIPS

WisdomWalks Principle
Pay attention to God's little nudges.

A man's conscience, like a warning line on the highway,
tells him what he shouldn't do—
but it does not keep him from doing it.

FRANK HOWARD CLARK

When I'm driving on the main roads and highways, I periodically experience that horrendously obnoxious, rattling vibration when I approach a toll booth or go outside the lines and hit those rumble strips. Depending on your car, you can experience a loud warning and tremendous tremors all the way through your steering wheel. Some even have reflectors, to add a visual warning. When I hit those rumble strips, they definitely get my attention. I often wonder if I'm going to blow a tire!

The most common reasons that drivers hit the rumble strips are fatigue or sleepiness, carelessness, inattentiveness, and distraction. By the way, did you know that driving while fatigued is compared with driving under the influence of alcohol? The same holds true for the use of cell phones that can now be used to call, text, and surf the Web.

While these rumble strips may seem incredibly annoying at the time, their "warnings" prevent accidents and literally save thousands of lives each year. I can't count the number of times *my* car has been rattled by them, and I've been jolted awake to avoid an accident.

Rumble strips have been installed on our roads for a good reason. Driving can be a blast, but it can also be dangerous.

Hmm…that sounds a lot like life, doesn't it?

Paul warned them, "Our voyage will be disastrous and bring great loss to ship and cargo, and to our own lives." But the centurion, instead of listening to Paul, followed the advice of the pilot and of the owner of the ship, and the majority decided to sail on. When a gentle south wind began to blow, they thought they had obtained what they wanted. Before very long, a wind of hurricane force swept down from the island. The ship was caught by the storm and driven along. We took such a violent battering that the next day they began to throw the cargo overboard, then the ship's tackle. Finally we gave up all hope of being saved.

ACTS 27:9–20 PARAPHRASED

This story gives a clear picture about what can happen when we ignore warnings. Paul, God's messenger and a prisoner, warned the crew not to sail. It was storm season. But the leaders were impatient, so they took a vote and decided to *ignore the warning* and *go along with the majority.* Their *immediate conditions improved,* so they were emboldened and convinced they chose the right path. But then *disaster struck*—a hurricane hit—and after a long fight they *gave in to it* and were *driven along,* completely out of control. The boat and crew *took a tremendous beating* and eventually *suffered great loss* as they threw their precious cargo overboard. Things got so bad they *gave up all hope* of being saved.

That sounds a lot like life, doesn't it? We're given warnings, but we ignore them, get beat up, and give up hope. What if we, instead, listened to those little nudges in our conscience? God works through warnings to:

Wake us up. Sometimes our defenses are down, and we don't realize the decisions we're making could lead to a big mistake. They seem innocent, even harmless, at the time. Other times we're blinded by emotions or think we're strong enough to handle the situation.

Keep us on track. The narrow road always leads to life. And God has an amazing adventure planned for us. Choosing detours that lead to destruction create delays and rob us of the relationship with Him that He desires.

Prevent a disaster for us and others around us. Our sins always affect more than just us. Somebody else gets hurt in the process. The military calls this *collateral damage*. Our actions always have far-reaching consequences.

God speaks to us in many ways: through our conscience, other people, the Holy Spirit, and the Word of God. Our ability to hear Him, discern His voice, and then obey His direction affects every aspect of our lives.

When I pay attention to the small "tweeks" in my conscience, I usually know the right thing to do. Then it's just a matter of doing it. But when I ignore His promptings, the answers He gives when I pray, or the advice of a close friend, it usually doesn't work out too well. Then I look back and think, *Why didn't I pay attention to all those signs? I could have avoided so much hardship.*

What rumble strips are you driving over in your life right now? Make no mistake, God is trying to get your attention.

Be a WisdomWalker!

Take a good look at the decisions you are making—the situations you put yourself in. Have you felt the jolt of rumble-strip warnings? If so, in what specific areas?

Why do you think God might be trying to get your attention?

A Step Deeper

Live Intentionally. Maximize Your Relationships. Pass the Torch.

Live It

1. Spend some time with God in prayer.
2. Ask God to reveal clearly to you any rumble strips you might be ignoring, being careless about, or being distracted from.
3. Write down everything He tells you in the "My Insights" section.
4. Confess any wrongdoing and sinful behavior and ask Him to forgive you.
5. Ask Him to give you the courage and determination to change what needs to be changed.

Maximize It

1. Talk with a trusted mentor about the rumble-strip warnings God has revealed to you. Ask if he or she sees any other areas of concern that should be addressed.
2. Why do you think God might be nudging you in these areas for your protection and benefit? Make a list together.
3. What changes could you make in your life this week to keep your tires on the road—and not bumping into the rumble strips?

Pass It On

For additional study, read and reflect on:

- Proverbs 29:1
- Luke 16:19–31
- Acts 2:36–41; 20:23
- Galatians 5:19–21

Share one of the above Scriptures with a friend or family member—and talk about how its wisdom and truth has influenced you to make some changes in your life.

My Insights

_____

_____

_____

_____

Father, examine my heart and my actions. Show me every part of my life—expose everything. Reveal to me the nudges in my conscience that I've ignored. Help me to hear Your voice, to feel the rattle from the rumble strips, and to make the changes necessary to stay on the road. Give me the focus and strength I need to follow Your direction for my life, not my own.

10

CAN YOU KEEP A SECRET?

WisdomWalks Principle
God rewards good deeds done behind the scenes.

The proud man raises his glass to toast himself,
blows the trumpet to tell of his greatness,
and writes his own headlines for all to read.
He praises himself for good deeds done,
but undoes the good deed by praising himself.

WILLIAM SHAKESPEARE (PARAPHRASED)

A lot has changed in the NFL in the last thirty years. In the 1980s, when players made a great play, they got right back in the huddle to get the next play; it was part of their job. In the 1990s, players would celebrate their own individual great play when it made a difference in the outcome of the game. But as the NFL stepped past the threshold of the year 2000, a different kind of attitude cropped up. Players now celebrate everything from a seven-yard catch to a first down to a great tackle, even if their team is losing by three touchdowns. Some even point to the name on the back of their jersey as they cross the goal line.

I have to admit, some of the players' antics are entertaining. But what's really going on here? It seems the days of selfless team ball are gone. It's now become "all about me."

I love team sports, and I love competition. And for a team to win, everybody on that team has to play their role and do their job. On my high school basketball team, we had guys who had to get rebounds, guards who had to distribute the ball, and shooters who could hit the shots. But everybody had to do the little things like box out, set picks, hustle, and play solid defense. The guys who averaged twenty points a game got a lot of the press, but they knew they couldn't score if everybody else just stood around.

Can you imagine what the game would look like if a player celebrated like crazy every time he set a solid pick? It would be complete chaos!

We all have a tendency to want to be seen, to be appreciated. We want people to think we're better than we really are. We want everyone to notice the good things we're doing. And we want the credit, too. But is that really what life's about? Or could there be something better?

WisdomWalking

Be careful not to do your acts of righteousness before men, to be seen by them. If you do, you will have no reward from your Father in heaven. So when you give to the needy, do not announce it with trumpets, as the hypocrites do in the synagogues and on the streets, to be honored by men…. And when you pray, do not be like the hypocrites, for they love to pray standing in the synagogues and on the street corners to be seen by men…. When you fast, do not look somber as the hypocrites do, for they disfigure their faces to show men they are fasting…. [Then your] Father, who sees what is done in secret, will reward you.

MATTHEW 6:1–2, 5, 16, 18

The truth is, trying to look good in front of others is an attitude rooted in pride. And because of our wrong motive, we turn what could be a good thing into a bad thing. When we seek the attention and praise of others, sure, we get our reward in the here and now (sometimes, at least). But when the applause ends, so does our reward.

However, doing good things in secret has eternal rewards. Jesus said in Matthew 6 to do good things—like pray, fast, and give—but to do them in secret. Even when Jesus performed miracles, He often told those He healed not to say anything. Why is that? Because the reward of "well done" from our heavenly Father is worth far more than any earthly reward ever could be. God rewards the good things we do in much greater ways than we could ever imagine—when we *don't* seek the credit for them.

Be a WisdomWalker!

Do you crave the limelight? Do you long for others' approval? If so, why? If not, why not? Is there something in your background or growing-up years that drives you to seek such attention now?

Do you tend to thank others for their help when you succeed, or do you take all the credit? Explain, using a recent event from your life.

How "public" are you about the good things you do (i.e., helping other people, giving to those in need, praying)? Could you continue to do some of these things—but in secret? Why or why not? What difference would doing them in secret make in your enjoyment of them?

A Step Deeper

Live Intentionally. Maximize Your Relationships. Pass the Torch.

Live It

1. Spend some time with God in prayer.
2. Ask God to reveal any areas of pride and craving for the limelight that you may have.
3. Write down everything He tells you in the "My Insights" section.
4. Confess any wrongdoing and sinful behavior and ask Him to forgive you.
5. Ask Him to give you the courage and determination to change what needs to be changed.

Maximize It

1. What one good deed could you do in secret this week? Perhaps these ideas can help get you started:
   a. Give—Bless someone who needs help financially with an anonymous gift.
   b. Serve—Drop off a surprise meal at someone's door.

    c. Pray—Intercede daily for someone going through a challenging time. Send anonymous, encouraging prayers.

    d. Fast—Abstain from food for a day and ask God to reveal ways for you to work behind-the-scenes to bless others.

    e. Thank—Privately express gratitude to others who have had a positive influence in your life.

2. Do your behind-the-scenes good deed, then write about your experience in your "My Insights" journal. How did it make you feel to do a good thing in secret? Did it help to keep your motive pure? Did it make you eager to do more?

Pass It On

For additional study, read and reflect on:

- Proverbs 27:2
- John 12:41–43
- Romans 2:29
- 2 Corinthians 10:15–18
- Galatians 1:10

Share one of the above Scriptures with a friend or family member—and talk about how its wisdom and truth has influenced you to make some changes in your life.

My Insights

_____

_____

_____

_____

Father, help me to seek Your pleasure rather than the praise of others. Expose the motives of my heart and reveal the ways I turn good things into bad because I want to be noticed. Give me opportunities to bless others anonymously. Help me to live more behind the scenes, knowing that my life will bear much fruit and that You reward the righteous things done in secret.

11

MR. IRRELEVANT

WisdomWalks Principle
There is greatness in everyone.

Expect great things from God,
attempt great things for God.

WILLIAM CAREY

Have you ever received a really special award for something you've done? If so, how did you feel the moment you received it? Now imagine you just received this award: Mr./Ms. Irrelevant. What would you think then?

Mr. Irrelevant is a real award. Since 1976, it's been given to the very last player selected in the NFL Draft. The 2009 Mr. Irrelevant award went to kicker Ryan Succop from the University of South Carolina. He was pick number 256 in the last round by the Kansas City Chiefs. He will even be given a trophy—the Lowsman Trophy, a spoof of the Heisman Trophy. This trophy actually depicts a player fumbling the ball! At the draft, Succop was even given an official NFL jersey with the number "256" and "Mr. Irrelevant" on the back.

Can you imagine getting tagged with the title Mr. Irrelevant? Basically, Mr. Not Important? I've been called many names over the years, but I'd struggle with that name. I don't like the idea that I'm not significant—that I don't count.

But Succop, a Christian and an active member of FCA on his college campus, has a very different outlook on his title. "I don't mind it," he says with a smile, "because I don't plan on being irrelevant. I plan on making an impact right away." I love it! Throw a "we're making fun of you" award and spoof trophy at him, but Succop still isn't about to get off track. He's grounded. He's got depth and wisdom.

FCA staff member Frank Hester says this about Succop's impact on his school: "Ryan is steady and consistent on and off the field. He loves the

Lord and gives Him all the credit for his talent and success. Ryan really tries to give back by speaking at local FCA Huddles and churches and by visiting sick children in the hospital."

Ryan Succop can't wait to have an impact in the NFL. God has already been preparing him for this so he can respond with power and might, not weakness. He has already plowed ministry ground in college, and he will do the same in Kansas City, no matter his "label." Succop isn't letting others define him.

Are you?

WisdomWalking

Get the word out. Teach all these things. And don't let anyone put you down because you're young. Teach believers with your life: by word, by demeanor, by love, by faith, by integrity.

1 TIMOTHY 4:11–12 MSG

The apostle Paul's letter to the young Timothy says it all: "Don't let anyone put you down." No matter what age or stage of life you're in, you can make a difference for Christ.

People might give Succop the title Mr. Irrelevant, but in God's eyes, he is Mr. Impact. In fact, to replace the jersey he received from the NFL, upon Succop's arrival in Kansas City, the FCA headquarters has an official jersey waiting for him with the number 1 and Mr. Impact on the back.

What about you? Are you planning for impact like Ryan Succop? Do you want the world to define who you are, or do you want the Lord Jesus Christ to define you?

Maybe you don't have the Lowsman Trophy on your shelf, but I'm sure from time to time you've felt irrelevant. Maybe you haven't received the credit you deserve at work, or certain friends don't hang out with you anymore, or you're exhausted from the stresses of everyday life, and you wonder, *Why am I doing this? Do I really matter?*

Instead of thinking of yourself as Mr./Ms. Irrelevant, why not try thinking of yourself as Mr./Ms. Impact instead? If you've joined God's team by believing and accepting Jesus Christ as Savior and Lord, you are already set apart for a great work in your home, your workplace, your community. You are set up for maximum impact. And, because Christ was victorious on the cross, you have already won.

So why not step out in faith? Who knows the incredible impact you'll have? (Actually, God does...and He's already smiling.)

Be a WisdomWalker!

When have you felt irrelevant or unimportant? How did you handle those feelings?

Have you ever been called a discouraging, ridiculous, or degrading name? How did you respond? What have you learned from Ryan Succop's response that might help you in similar situations in the future?

Is it hard for you to not dwell on the "bad stuff" that happens? Why or why not? How can you begin dwelling on the good instead?

A Step Deeper

Live Intentionally. Maximize Your Relationships. Pass the Torch.

Live It

1. Spend some time with God in prayer.
2. Ask God to reveal to you any areas where you feel irrelevant but long to make an impact.
3. Write down everything He tells you in the "My Insights" section.
4. Confess any wrongdoing and sinful behavior and ask Him to forgive you.
5. Ask Him to give you the courage and determination to change what needs to be changed.

Maximize It

1. Talk to a trusted friend about the areas where you feel irrelevant. Share your heart's desires about dreams and goals you have about making a difference.
2. Talk about what being "already victorious" means. How can that understanding help you move ahead in your desires to make an impact?
3. Form a plan of one event where you can make a difference...and step out in faith.

Pass It On

For additional study, read and reflect on:

- Romans 12

Share one or two verses from the above Scripture passage with a friend or family member—and talk about how its wisdom and truth has influenced you to make some changes in your life.

My Insights

_____

_____

_____

_____

_____

_____

Lord Jesus, how I long to make an impact on those around me! When it comes to the kingdom, the last thing I want to be is irrelevant. Help me, Jesus, to have an awesome attitude like Ryan's. Put a sense of urgency in my heart to become a person of impact. Thank You, Lord, that I have victory because You have already won. In Jesus' name I pray. Amen.

12

PRAY LIKE BIRDIE

WisdomWalks Principle
Prayer does change things.

*To be a Christian without prayer is no more possible
than to be alive without breathing.*

MARTIN LUTHER

Birdie Pitts served Christ for all of her ninety-two years on earth. Twenty years ago, she was my first official prayer warrior. Little did I know at that time, however, that Birdie had actually started praying for me eleven years before that.

I was in eighth grade when I first met two buddies, James and Tim (Birdie's grandson), at a summer camp in New York. Not only did I make two lifetime friends at that camp, but I also made a commitment to full-time ministry. When I returned from camp, I met Birdie, and she started to pray for me, her grandson's new best friend.

Birdie prayed for Tim, James, and me faithfully that God would use us significantly for His glory. We're convinced her years of prayer shaped and transformed the three of us. Tim became a youth pastor, James became a missionary in Hungary, and I came on staff with Fellowship of Christian Athletes. It was evidence of a powerful God and the faithful intercession of His saint, Birdie.

On August 9, 2001, Birdie went home to be with the Lord. While attending her funeral, I thought about how many lives she'd touched through her prayers. Birdie was not only faithful in prayer, but also faithful to ensure that I gave her specific prayer requests. If she hadn't heard from me, she'd phone to say, "I haven't received any prayer requests from you this month. The ladies are gathering tomorrow for prayer. You don't need prayer this month?" She truly kept me on my toes. The highlight for me was when she would have me over to her apartment for her prayer group. After a quick update and sharing of specific requests, we prayed. No idle talk or chit-chat. We got down to business. We were there to pray, and pray we did!

Birdie was serious about prayer. She carved out the time needed to call upon the Lord for others. She knew about prayers of strength and length. She wrestled with God, and doors were opened. Hearts were moved. Lives were transformed. And still Birdie pressed on.

WisdomWalking

Be joyful in hope, patient in affliction, faithful in prayer.

ROMANS 12:12

When I picture someone faithful in prayer, Birdie is the first person who comes to mind. It seems like many people today use the "…like Jesus" phrase. Lead like Jesus. Serve like Jesus. Pray like Jesus. Jesus modeled prayer to His disciples and even taught them to pray. I've studied the Scriptures to learn why and how to pray, but it's hard for me to truly know what it is like to pray like Jesus. But I do know what it means to "pray like Birdie." During those twenty years she was my prayer warrior, I watched and studied how she prayed. Here is what I learned:

- Be consistent. Set a regular prayer time—daily, weekly, and monthly.
- Be persistent. Pursue prayer with others. Don't let prayer fall between the cracks.
- Be specific. Dig into the nitty-gritty. Don't be general. God loves details.
- Be faithful. Show up! Others are counting on your prayers.
- Be prayerful. Don't talk, pray! Get down to business.

When I think about Birdie, I'm reminded of Leonard Ravenhill's famous quote about prayer: "The church has many organizers, but few agonizers. Many resters, but few wrestlers. Many who are enterprising, but few who are interceding. People who are not praying are playing. In the matter of effective praying, never have so many left so much to so few." Birdie will forever be a part of why I am in ministry, and I am grateful for the hundreds of hours she invested before the throne of grace on my behalf. She truly was a prayer warrior, and she changed more lives than she knew.

I wonder how many people count on your prayers—not on what you can do for them, but how you can pray for them. Why not pray like Birdie?

Be a WisdomWalker!

Do you have a Birdie in your life? If so, describe her/him. How have those prayers—and that person's belief in you—influenced your own belief and actions?

How important is prayer to you personally? Do you set aside time each day to pray? Why or why not? If so, how do you accomplish that? If not, today's a good day to begin to pray like Birdie!

Have you seen the power of prayer at work in your life? If so, tell the story!

A Step Deeper

Live Intentionally. Maximize Your Relationships. Pass the Torch.

Live It

1. Spend some time with God in prayer.
2. Ask God to help you pray like Birdie—with determination and focus.
3. Write down everything He tells you in the "My Insights" section.
4. Confess any wrongdoing and sinful behavior and ask Him to forgive you.
5. Ask Him to give you the courage and determination to change what needs to be changed.

Maximize It

1. Discuss with a trusted friend what it means to be faithful in prayer. (See Romans 12:12.)
2. Talk about Leonard Ravenhill's quote. Do you tend to be an organizer or an agonizer? A rester or a wrestler? Explain.

3. How can you pray like Birdie? Which of these five prayer principles is easiest for you? Hardest? How can you incorporate them into your heart, mind, and life?
   a. Be consistent.
   b. Be persistent.
   c. Be specific.
   d. Be faithful.
   e. Be prayerful.

Pass It On

For additional study, read and reflect on:

- Isaiah 59:1
- Romans 12:12
- Colossians 4:3
- 2 Timothy 1:7

Share one of the above Scriptures with a friend or family member—and talk about how its wisdom and truth has influenced you to make some changes in your life.

My Insights

_____

_____

_____

_____

Father, thank You for the blessing of prayer. Sometimes I admit that prayer is hard. My mind races through other things, and it is difficult to stay focused. Help me not to waiver. I desire to lay hold of the treasures of heaven, such as hope, peace, joy, and purpose. Teach me to pray, Lord. I want to impact others through my prayer life. I know people are counting on my prayers. Help me to be consistent, persistent, specific, faithful, and prayerful—like Birdie. In the name of Jesus I pray. Amen.

13

DIG IN

WisdomWalks Principle
A step of faith often means "stay," not "go."

*I could not at any age be content to take my place
in a corner by the fireside and simply look on.
Life was meant to be lived.
You must do the thing you think you cannot do.*

ELEANOR ROOSEVELT

L et me ask you a question: if you could have one incredible year, packed full of recognition and awards, or a lifetime filled with good, solid, consistent performances, what would you choose?

How you answer that challenging question reveals just how you're wired. Are you the type of person who looks for the next big opportunity, or someone who digs in right where you are and accomplishes what needs to be done? In today's world, authors jump from publisher to publisher, singing stars change recording companies, and fathers leave their families to pursue younger women. The grass always looks greener on the other side of the fence, doesn't it? That's why many of us are so quick to pursue the next big, great opportunity.

So many people say they want to be used by God, but they never take time to develop relationships or to dig into the powerful community that God wants to give them. Instead, they switch jobs, cities, and schools before they even ask God, *Is there something you want me to be doing right here?*

We all have our own personal agendas, and sometimes we let those take over, rather than listening to the still voice of God. We rush to make a move, to change the current dynamic. But God is looking for a few good men, women, and children who will dig in where they're planted and be consistent. He wants the faithful, not the flashy. He wants someone who is sold out, not a sell-out. He wants someone who is persistent, not prosperous. Patient, not popular.

Which kind of person are you?

"The kingdom of God is like this," He said. "A man scatters seed on the ground; he sleeps and rises—night and day, and the seed sprouts and grows—he doesn't know how. The soil produces a crop by itself—first the blade, then the head, and then the ripe grain on the head. But as soon as the crop is ready, he sends for the sickle, because harvest has come."

MARK 4:26-29 HCSB

The father in these verses is certainly industrious. He's committed to doing the work day and night. And, because he's willing to pay the price of consistency and determination, he reaps a great harvest. It just takes time.

It's amazing how God can use you if you commit to staying put. You'll grow where God plants you…if you give it time. That kind of consistency is important to reaping the harvest.

Consistency is extremely important to me. Each day I do a gut-check to make sure I'm committed to engaging the world right in the place where God has put me. If each of us keeps putting our "hand to the plow" and not looking back (or around), imagine what we could get done! How greatly God could use us!

I'm continually amazed at how God has used someone like me, and I'm convinced it's because of consistency. I went to the same high school all four years; I spent four years at the same college. I played for the same professional lacrosse team my entire pro career. I've been on staff at FCA for eighteen years. I dated my wife for nine years before we married, and now we've been married for eighteen years. With each season of my life, God showed up powerfully, and I was in awe. Sure, I had opportunities that looked bigger and better, but I just kept showing up right where I was—with unwavering commitment. And so did God!

So here's my challenge to you: Commit for the long haul. Don't bail. Be faithful. Be consistent. Dig in and make a difference. Then get ready for God's surprises.

Be a WisdomWalker!

When was the last time you committed to something for the long haul? How did God use you through that experience?

Are you more prone to digging in or taking off? Why?

How could God use you in your current situation (home, school, work, community) if you are willing to dig in?

A Step Deeper

Live Intentionally. Maximize Your Relationships. Pass the Torch.

Live It

1. Spend some time with God in prayer.
2. Ask God to help you be consistent and commit for the long haul.
3. Write down everything He tells you in the "My Insights" section.
4. Confess any wrongdoing and sinful behavior and ask Him to forgive you.
5. Ask Him to give you the courage and determination to change what needs to be changed.

Maximize It

1. Andy Stanley defines big faith as being "when our faith intersects God's faithfulness." What do you think he means? Discuss the quote with a friend. How does Stanley's quote apply to digging in to where you are now?

2. What is one area of your life in which you could be more consistent? How could you go about doing that?
3. Ask a trusted friend to hold you accountable "for the long haul" in that area.

Pass It On
For additional study, read and reflect on:

- Galatians 6:9
- 2 Thessalonians 3:13

Share one of the above Scriptures with a friend or family member—and talk about how its wisdom and truth has influenced you to make some changes in your life.

My Insights

_____

_____

_____

_____

_____

_____

_____

Lord Jesus, I ask for Your help in developing consistency. I want to dig in, Jesus, and be counted for the long haul. I believe that You, Lord, have a plan to do a mighty work through me, and I know You are able. As opportunities come my way, give me the wisdom to know if they are distractions from man or opportunities from You. I ask for a big faith, Lord, and I desire to be marked by commitment and faithfulness. In Jesus' name I pray. Amen.

14

OPPORTUNITY KNOCKS...

WisdomWalks Principle
Guard yourself, because temptation lurks.

*The reason so many people never get anywhere in life
is because when opportunity knocks,
they are out in the backyard looking for four-leaf clovers.*

WALTER P. CHRYSLER

We all know what it means to be at the right place at the right time. Each of us has stories about when opportunity came knocking. I heard the knock when I was drafted to play professional lacrosse after graduating from college. Looking back on it, I was simply at the right place at the right time. The conditions were perfect: the team needed my abilities, and the coach liked my style of play. I probably wouldn't have made any other team in the league, but I was at the right place at the right time, so I seized the opportunity.

Over time, I've learned that there are good opportunities, and there are bad opportunities. Just like you can be at the right place at the right time, you can also be at the wrong place at the wrong time. Unfortunately, I found myself opening the door to some of these, too. (Haven't you? Those times when you say to yourself, *How did I get myself into this mess? What just happened? I sure didn't plan on this.*) Even now, I have a knot in my stomach, thinking back on some of the bad opportunities that sprang out of nowhere. Sometimes I simply wasn't cautious enough—or smart enough—to say no.

I find comfort, though, in knowing I'm not the first person to fall for a bad opportunity. I've got some good company from way back. King David—"the man after God's own heart"—experienced this kind of opportunity, and he chose unwisely. When all of the other kings went off to battle, David stayed home. His decision to ignore his responsibility to go to war with his troops gave rise to a bad opportunity to connect with the beautiful Bathsheba. David was at the wrong place at the wrong time. If he'd been doing what he was supposed to be doing, there was a good chance he wouldn't have fallen.

When you're doing what you're supposed to do, the seemingly endless responsibilities, appointments, meetings, and daily routines actually offer you many sin-safeguards. By going through these time-consuming and relatively mundane motions, you're protected from a host of opportunities to sin. It's when you "float," like David did, that the bad opportunities raise their ugly heads.

Bad opportunities always come when your guard is down. Satan loves to surprise and ambush you. And he's really, really good at it. But that doesn't mean you have to fall for the bad opportunities.

WisdomWalking

If you do right, won't you be accepted? But if you do not do right, sin is crouching at the door. Its desire is for you, but you must master it.

GENESIS 4:7 HCSB

If you don't use your free time wisely, there can be great temptation to sin. Mindless channel-surfing gives rise to hundreds of opportunities to see stuff you didn't want to see. Several hours on the Web and you'll discover sites you had no intention of visiting. You might not have been looking for bad opportunities, but they popped up right there on the screen.

As God said to Cain, "Sin is crouching at the door." *Crouching* means "waiting for the perfect opportunity to spring." So what can you do? You can be on guard. You can build in safeguards (such as what Billy Graham did—he refused to be alone with another woman other than his wife) and use time wisely, instead of wasting it. If you're fulfilled and satisfied with your life and the way it's going, you'll be less likely to jump at a bad opportunity.

Before you open the door of opportunity, you'd be wise to take a good, long look at it through the peephole first.

Be a WisdomWalker!

Have you ever been surprised by a bad opportunity? What happened as a result? Tell the story.

When do you find yourself drawn into bad opportunities? Is there a pattern you can identify that could help you spot such opportunities in the future?

In what area(s) of your life might a bad opportunity be crouching at your door right now? Be specific about the potential temptation. Why would this temptation, in particular, be difficult for you to turn down? Explain.

A Step Deeper

Live Intentionally. Maximize Your Relationships. Pass the Torch.

Live It

1. Spend some time with God in prayer.
2. Ask God to reveal to you any bad opportunities—both now and in the future.
3. Write down everything He tells you in the "My Insights" section.
4. Confess any wrongdoing and sinful behavior and ask Him to forgive you.
5. Ask Him to give you the courage and determination to change what needs to be changed.

Maximize It

1. Before you act on an opportunity, talk it through with a trusted mentor. Is this a good opportunity? A bad opportunity? How can you tell? What criteria will you use?
2. Tell a trusted friend about the bad opportunity crouching at your door right now. Brainstorm how you can keep yourself out of harm's way

both in this situation and in future similar situations. Pray together, asking God to give you strength to master the temptation.

3. Discuss how you can be intentional about the opportunities you choose. What safeguards can you put into your life? How can you keep bad opportunities *outside* your door, rather than inside, where they can do you great harm?

Pass It On

For additional study, read and reflect on:

- 2 Samuel 11:1–5
- James 1:13–17
- 1 Peter 5:8

Share one of the above Scriptures with a friend or family member—and talk about how its wisdom and truth has influenced you to make some changes in your life.

My Insights

_____

_____

_____

_____

_____

_____

Jesus, I ask for the wisdom to discern the difference between good and bad opportunities. When bad opportunities arise, Your Word says we must be prepared and stand firm. I do not want to fall or stumble. I do not want to be deceived. So please, Lord, order my footsteps. May my time and schedule be glorifying to You. Let me not waste time in activities that would open the door to unwise opportunities. Today, with Your help, I choose to keep sin outside the door! Thank You, Jesus. Amen.

15

THE BIGGEST GIVER

WisdomWalks Principle
Give deeply of yourself, and you'll never go wrong.

Only one life, 'twill soon be past,
only what's done for Christ will last.

CHARLES THOMAS STUDD
(MISSIONARY TO CHINA, INDIA, AND AFRICA)

Stephen Paletta is a special guy in more ways than one. In April 2008, he was announced in the finale episode of the first season of Oprah Winfrey's ABC reality show *Big Give* as "The Biggest Giver." He'd made it through eight episodes and survived the competition of nine other big-hearted contestants. But that's only the tip of the iceberg regarding Stephen's big heart.

I first met Stephen in 1992, when I was doing one of my favorite things: playing lacrosse in a summer tournament in Vail, Colorado. Sixteen teams were competing. During the tournament and our team's run to the championship, I became friends with this tough-playing defenseman, who had the rare combination of a competitive drive and a caring heart. He was a teammate who cared for others and actively looked for ways to bless people.

During that lacrosse tournament, God got a hold of Stephen in a deeper way. Even though Stephen already had a big heart, he realized he still needed God's heart. Reflecting back on that experience, Stephen says it was an "aha" moment in his life. "Those four days changed everything. The games were miraculous, to say the least. At that point I said, 'Okay, God, I guess You got me.'"

Since then, I've been privileged to watch his heart for God grow. And I've learned a hefty life principle: there's nothing like the heat of competition to show your true colors. It's hard to hide your heart when you are sweating and giving a game your all. Everything within you comes out; sports have a way of exposing the truth for all to see. Since that '92 lacrosse tournament, Stephen's Christ-like influence has had a major impact in the lives of many athletes and coaches. He's a man who knows what it means to serve with a heart yielded to Christ.

So, when Oprah's *Big Give* show opportunity came along, Stephen approached it with that same attitude. "I had no idea what I was going to do," he said. "Each morning I'd wake up and say, 'All right God, just let me know what I need to know today.' I went into the show with a servant's heart. 'God, whatever it is You want me to do with these folks, let it happen. I'm just going to be here to do my very best.' At no time did I think about the competition. At no time did I think I could win this thing. I simply considered myself very fortunate to be connected to these people in need." During the show, Stephen's heart was revealed. Everyone saw how he not only met needs but cared for others. His love for people naturally flowed from his heart.

That's what big, deep giving is all about.

WisdomWalking

So I will very gladly spend for you everything I have and expend myself as well.

2 CORINTHIANS 12:15

To serve others and to give of yourself is true worship. Oswald Chambers once said, "Worship is giving God the best that He has given you. Whenever you get a blessing from God, give it back to Him as a love gift." What Stephen does best is bless others because his heart is full of God's love. On the playing field or off the playing field, he is a walking, talking, living example of Christ. People might define him as the "Biggest Giver," but the Lord defines him simply as an obedient follower of Christ.

Be a WisdomWalker!

Why do you think the heart is the main factor in how big someone gives?

Would those who know you tag you as someone with a big heart? Why or why not?

What does Paul mean when he writes in 2 Corinthians 12:15, "So I will gladly spend for you everything I have and expend myself as well"? Why is this natural or unnatural for you?

What gets in your way of being able to see and meet other people's needs and hearts? How can you position yourself to serve at a greater level?

A Step Deeper

Live Intentionally. Maximize Your Relationships. Pass the Torch.

Live It

1. Spend some time with God in prayer.
2. Ask God to enlarge your heart toward others so you will gladly give of yourself and your resources.
3. Write down everything He tells you in the "My Insights" section.
4. Confess any wrongdoing and sinful behavior and ask Him to forgive you.
5. Ask Him to give you the courage and determination to change what needs to be changed.

Maximize It

1. Talk with a trusted friend about how you could grow God's heart in your

heart. List some specific ways you could both "spend and expend" yourself.

2. How could you become a walking, talking example of Christ in your home, your workplace, your school, your community?

3. Follow through on one brainstorm from your list in the next week.

Pass It On

For additional study, read and reflect on:

- Acts 4:32
- 1 Thessalonians 4:11–12
- 1 Timothy 6:18

Share one of the above Scriptures with a friend or family member—and talk about how its wisdom and truth has influenced you to make some changes in your life.

My Insights

_____

_____

_____

_____

_____

_____

_____

_____

Lord Jesus, I ask for a big heart so I can be a blessing. Help me, Lord, to focus on others and not on myself. May You be glorified when I return to You what You have given to me. Help me to have a heart that is yielded to You. Show me what it means to be rich in good deeds. I want to be able to live as Paul lived, gladly spending everything for others: my money, abilities, and blessings. May all who see me define me simply as an obedient follower of You.

16

IMAGE IS EVERYTHING!

WisdomWalks Principle
Make your reputation match your reality.

Character is like a tree and reputation like a shadow.
The shadow is what we think of it; the tree is the real thing.
ABRAHAM LINCOLN

I admit it. I fell right in the advertisers' trap...once (okay, more than once) when a leading camera company named Canon aired a television commercial with the catchy tagline, "Image is Everything!™" In the commercial, tennis pro Andre Agassi was cranking serves and backhands, driving in a Jeep with the doors off, and wearing trendy clothes. The commercials were so effective that I actually bought one of their cameras.

The truth is, the images this camera takes are spectacular! But we all know that a camera can't capture what's really going on inside. It can only capture what we want it to—what we are willing to let it see. It can't capture character. The outward image can be amazing even when the inward reality is in turmoil. And most of us like to project the appearance that everything is fine.

When I graduated from college and got a decent job, I bought my first car—a bright red sports car—within thirty days. I originally chose a black one, but when I went in to pick it up, I decided to go with the red one. Then I bought a couple of expensive suits with trendy ties (and even suspenders). I bought a pair of glasses even though I had perfect vision! You see, I wanted to project a certain image. At the time, I had the appearance of success. Interestingly, simultaneously I got involved in the church and other ministries as a volunteer and became known as a person of solid faith and character.

But I discovered later that I was full of pride. I was selfish. Just about everything I did centered on creating the appearance that I had it all together. I was even driven to succeed to keep the image intact. But I lacked genuine peace and joy. I was easily angered, frustrated, and defensive, but few people saw that part of me. Yet I certainly was not reflecting the image of God.

You clean the outside of the cup and dish, but inside [you] are full of greed and self-indulgence.... First clean the inside of the cup and dish, and then the outside also will be clean.... You are like whitewashed tombs, which look beautiful on the outside but on the inside are full of dead men's bones and everything unclean. In the same way, on the outside you appear to people as righteous but on the inside you are full of hypocrisy and wickedness.

MATTHEW 23:25–28

When I read these verses, they hit me between the eyes. When the inside doesn't match the outside, Jesus calls that *hypocrisy.* And that's what I was—a hypocrite. Just like the Pharisees, the religious leaders of the day, who had the appearance of righteousness but inside were corrupt. They would make a huge show about cleaning the outside of the cup and dish so they wouldn't be tainted by anyone else's germs or unworthiness, but if you got up close and got to know them, you'd never want to drink out of or eat off those dishes! The Pharisees' hearts were selfish. They were driven by power and position, and they enjoyed feeling like they were better than everybody else. They created a great public image, but they did not reflect the image of God.

We're all concerned with image, to one degree or another, aren't we? We want to appear better than we really are, and we're careful to let people only see our best. Yet while we protect our reputation, Jesus sees our reality.

What He cares about is the condition of your heart. Do you love Him? Do you love others? Are your motives pure? Are you driven to project and protect your image, or are you passionate about reflecting and revealing who He really is?

Everything Jesus did on earth reflected the image of His Father. Everything you do—both outside and inside—should reflect Jesus. To Him, *image is everything*—because He wants to change you on the inside into the likeness of God.

At the end of the day, my goal is to be able to say I've followed the words of 1 Chronicles 29:17: "I know, my God, that you test the heart and are pleased with integrity." How about you?

Be a WisdomWalker!

What kind of an image do you project to others? Be specific.

What things do you say and do to create that image? Why is projecting that image important to you?

In what way(s) does this image reflect who you are on the inside—or not reflect who you are on the inside? How do you handle the tension between your reputation and your reality?

A Step Deeper

Live Intentionally. Maximize Your Relationships. Pass the Torch.

Live It

1. Spend some time with God in prayer.
2. Examine the condition of your heart. Ask Jesus to reveal to you what things need to change so your reputation matches your reality.
3. Write down everything He tells you in the "My Insights" section.
4. Confess any wrongdoing and sinful behavior and ask Him to forgive you.
5. Ask Him to give you the courage and determination to change what needs to be changed.

Maximize It

1. If what you are like on the inside now suddenly appeared on the outside, what do you think people would see? Are you comfortable with that image? Why, or why not?

2. The next time you're doing dishes, take a dirty cup and dish out of the sink. Carefully clean the outside of the cup and the underside of the dish, leaving the inside of both dirty. Then take a good, long look. If you only saw the outside of the cup and dish, would you want to eat out of them? Would you change your mind if you saw the inside? How does a glimpse of what's on the inside make a difference?

3. Look at your "My Insights" notes. What key areas of your life need to change so that your reputation matches your reality? How will you begin to change these areas?

Pass It On

For additional study, read and reflect on:

- Genesis 1:26–27
- Mark 7:14–23
- Luke 11:42–52

Share one of the above Scriptures with a friend or family member—and talk about how its wisdom and truth has influenced you to make some changes in your life.

My Insights

_____

_____

_____

_____

_____

Father, I know You see my heart, my attitudes, my unspoken thoughts, my spoken words, and my emotions. You see me when no one else does. You know the real me. I ask for Your help, Lord. I want to change. Reveal to me the things in my character that need to change so I can bear Your image and become more and more like Jesus. Amen.

17

IDENTITY THEFT

WisdomWalks Principle
Reclaim the real you.

i·den·ti·ty (ī'dentitē) noun
[1] the set of behavioral or personal characteristics by which
an individual is recognizable as a member of a group.
[2] the distinct personality of an individual.

> *When you know **who you are**,*
> *then you'll know **how to live**.*
> JIMMY PAGE

I dentity theft is a big thing in our world today. That means somebody has taken your name and key information about you, such as your address, birthday, social security number, or even account numbers, and pretended to be you. Did you know that, in America alone, 8.4 million adults have their identity stolen every year? That's sixteen people every single minute of every day! Worse yet, the average identity theft results in $5,720 in illegal purchases!

In today's culture, a name has very little importance. When we're choosing names for our kids, most of us just choose names we like. We don't realize that every name has a meaning or, if we do, we're more concerned with how the name sounds or how it fits together with our last name.

But in ancient times, names had weight. They had implications for your very identity. Often they spoke to the character and integrity of the person and illuminated some characteristic of God. Such is the story of Daniel and his friends from the famous account from the lions' den.

Then the king ordered Ashpenaz, chief of his court officials, to bring in some of the Israelites from the royal family and the nobility—young men without any physical defect, handsome, showing aptitude for every kind of learning, well informed, quick to understand, and qualified to serve in the king's palace. He was to teach them the language and literature of the Babylonians.... Among these were Daniel, Hananiah, Mishael, and Azariah.

DANIEL 1:3–4, 6–7 PARAPHRASED

When the four Israelite young men were chosen for the Babylonian king Nebuchadnezzar's service, their names and entire identities had to be changed. After all, *Daniel* means "God is my judge"; *Hananiah,* "The Lord"; *Mishael,* "Who is what God is?"; *Azariah,* "The Lord helps." The pagan king certainly didn't want a reminder that he wasn't God—especially since the entire purpose of the training program was to transform Jews into Babylonians in every way possible. So, in order to make the identity theft complete, Nebuchadnezzar changed their names.

But the king's plan didn't quite work the way he thought. Even though he fully indoctrinated these young men into Babylonian culture, since they were completely devoted to God, their hearts and true identities were untouchable. Eventually they took their stand for the one true God to face the lions and the fiery furnace.

If you are a Christian, you've had your original identity restored. The sin that stole your true identity, separating you from God, has been cleansed by the blood of Jesus Christ on the cross. Now you have a new identity—not only in name, but throughout your entire being, as only God can do.

When you place your faith in Jesus, you become *a new creation.* The old identity passes away, and the new identity emerges. Is the process complete? No. But it has begun. God's transformational work is underway. You've been set free from your sin and can now become everything God designed you to be. You have the power to take a stand and live differently from the rest of the corrupt culture around you.

Also, if you believe in His name, you've been given the right to be called His *child*. That means you've been adopted by God, and you take on *His* name! But better still, your heart, mind, thoughts, and attitudes have been changed too. Since you are now part of God's family, how you live will affect everyone else in the family.

Finally, you've been given His *character*. When God the Father sees you now, He sees the righteousness of Christ. And when you act in a way that's inconsistent with His character, He'll prompt you to get back on track. That's because you no longer live—it is Christ living in you.

Now that's an identity and a "real you" that will stand firm for all eternity!

Be a WisdomWalker!

Write three personal characteristics from your driver's license that describe you. Do any reveal the real you—the type of person you are or your true character? Why or why not?

Write three things that tell the "inside story" of who you are—your true identity. Are these consistent with the person God made you to be?

What does it mean that you have become a "new creation"? List three things that God has changed in you since you believed in Him.

A Step Deeper

Live Intentionally. Maximize Your Relationships. Pass the Torch.

Live It

1. Spend some time with God in prayer.
2. Ask God to reveal to you any "old identity" habits that cause problems for you.
3. Write down everything He tells you in the "My Insights" section.
4. Confess any wrongdoing and sinful behavior and ask Him to forgive you.
5. Ask Him to give you the courage and determination to change what needs to be changed.

Maximize It

1. What can you celebrate about your new identity in Christ? What from your old identity is still troublesome? What's the biggest thing you want God's help to change?
2. What does it mean to belong to God's family? How does that affect your perspective of your identity?
3. Can you grow the character of Christ? If so, how? And how would that change the way you live?

Pass It On

For additional study, read and reflect on:

- 2 Corinthians 5:17
- Galatians 2:20
- Ephesians 1:5
- 1 John 3:1

Share one of the above Scriptures with a friend or family member—and talk about how its wisdom and truth has influenced you to make some changes in your life.

My Insights

_____

_____

_____

_____

_____

Father, help me realize I'm much more than just something You've created. I am Your child—part of your family. And the moment I put my faith in Jesus, You made me new. I am no longer a slave to sin or my old habits, but I have been given the character of Christ. Give me the power and strength I need to stand against the culture and reveal my true identity.

18

3 – D

WisdomWalks Principle
Engage God daily—no matter what!

*How much of your life you've invested in Jesus Christ is the issue.
Have we held some back for ourselves—just in case He's not as real, as powerful,
as active as we thought? Just in case He doesn't come through?
Just in case He really can't be taken at His Word?
Or have we banked everything we have and everything we are
on the reality that Jesus Christ is Lord of all the earth?
We will never fulfill our destinies until our hope is built on nothing less.*

BETH MOORE, *BELOVED DISCIPLE*

My dad loved to engage God daily. He was a passionate man who delighted in challenging people to have a daily quiet time. Even though he passed away in 2008 after a long fight with leukemia, his passion has impacted thousands. He was the kind of guy who, if he met you for the first time and had just one minute with you to communicate one thing, he would address your personal quiet time. It was a passion that overflowed from him because it was such an essential part of his life. But it had not always been that way. Eighteen years earlier, he was an overcommitted businessman who would squeeze in a quick, two-minute devotion in his car before he ran into his office to start the day.

That all changed with the help of Brad Curl, a good friend of my dad's. When Brad saw that my dad, who served on many local ministry boards, was skimming when it came to his devotions, Brad decided to communicate with him in a way that got his attention. Brad literally grabbed my dad by the collar, put him against the wall, and said, "Ed, you need to stop playing with God. You are a Christian leader, and you need to start diving into God's Word and getting serious! No more giving God leftovers!"

As a very intense person himself, my dad responded to this style of communication. That day marked my dad. No more quick devos. He started digging in. He began feasting on God's Word first thing every morning, and his life began to transform. As he spent time in the Bible, the Bible got into him.

WisdomWalking

May Your hand be ready to help me, for I have chosen Your precepts. I long for Your salvation, LORD, and Your instruction is my delight. Let me live, and I will praise You; may Your judgments help me.

PSALM 119:173–175 HCSB

My dad always shared the 3–Ds of Devotions: Drudgery, Discipline, and Delight. He would say, "You have to start today. Don't wait until tomorrow. If you do it now, you have won! Getting up daily and doing a quiet time starts out as drudgery. You won't like it, but you just do it. It is hard and unnatural, but you just get it done. Then, gradually, it grows into a discipline. You begin to realize that it is important, and you need to do it. It becomes a part of the way you do life. Then, if you stay at it long enough, it will become a delight. You love it and desire to do it. You can't wait to do it because you long to be with the Lord. It is an opportunity to meet the God of the universe each day. It is a joy to be with the Savior. Why would you ever want to pass up a daily uninterrupted, intimate time with God? It goes from a 'have-to' to a 'need-to' to a 'want-to.'"

I've experienced firsthand how right my dad was about the power of spending time in devotions. Although my dad is now in heaven, his message lives on through me, and I'm now delighting in sharing it with others. What thrills me the most is when I see lives transform as a result.

Jesus Christ is waiting today to empower you with His presence. He longs to be with you. Why not engage God today? Yes, it's hard, but it's worth it. Stay with it until it becomes a delight. I get fired up knowing that no matter what D stage I'm at, it's a delight for the Lord Jesus Christ every day when I choose to engage Him. He longs to be with you and me much more than we long to be with Him. Oh, how He loves you and me!

Be a WisdomWalker!

On a scale of 1 (no devotions) to 10 (devotions is a huge focus in your life), where would you rate yourself? Why?

Which D stage best defines your current quiet time? Explain.

What gets in the way of making devotions a part of your life? Make a list of these "blockers" that prevent you from getting into the Word. How could you step around one of these blockers to make time for God this week?

A Step Deeper

Live Intentionally. Maximize Your Relationships. Pass the Torch.

Live It

1. Spend some time with God in prayer.
2. Ask God to help you "get in the zone" with Him each day.
3. Write down everything He tells you in the "My Insights" section.
4. Confess any wrongdoing and sinful behavior and ask Him to forgive you.
5. Ask Him to give you the courage and determination to change what needs to be changed.

Maximize It

1. Who in your life can speak truth into you, as Brad Curl did for my dad? In trying to effect change in your life, accountability is key. Approach

this person and ask if he or she would hold you accountable with check-ins every week, to see how you're doing.

2. Read Psalm 119 and circle how many times the word *delight* is used. Why do you think God would use this word to describe His words?

3. God delights in you every time you engage Him. It's never drudgery or discipline for Him. How could this perspective of God encourage you in your pursuit of daily devotions?

Pass It On
For additional study, read and reflect on:

- Psalm 1:2; 35:9
- Isaiah 42:16

Share one of the above Scriptures with a friend or family member—and talk about how its wisdom and truth has influenced you to make some changes in your life.

My Insights

_____

_____

_____

_____

_____

_____

_____

Jesus, I desire to be with You every day. I want to be in Your presence. My soul longs and thirsts for You. Help me to carve out the time each day to hear from You. I know You delight in me when I engage You, but I want to delight in You. Transform my quiet times so they go from drudgery to discipline to pure delight. In Your name I pray. Amen.

19

THE SNOWBALL EFFECT

WisdomWalks Principle
Little things always become big things.

*The journey of a thousand miles
begins with a single step.*
CHINESE PROVERB

There are two kinds of people in the world—those who love snow, and those who hate it. I've seen my share of snow in my life, and I love it! This week alone dumped over fifty inches of snow on our region, causing a shutdown of major airports and major power outages.

Just before the storm hit, I was on my *Fit Life Today* radio program, giving tips for how to survive the storm. One of the tips was to clear the snow a little at a time instead of waiting until a foot accumulated. Why risk injury via shoveling by letting the snow build up? "My boys and I will be out every two hours to clear the snow," I said. "We'll do the little things along the way so we can avoid the heavy work of trying to remove two feet all at once."

Well, our intentions were good, but then bedtime came along. By morning the accumulation was over twenty inches. We felt so overwhelmed that, instead of getting right on it before it got worse, we let it snow for another five hours before we got out the shovels.

Some people call this "The Law of Accumulation," but I call it "The Snowball Effect." Little things lead to big things. A little snowball turns into a giant snowman. Small steps lead to giant leaps. Every decision, every action, every thought, and every word counts. And while we don't necessarily see the effect at each moment along the way, the little things we do (or don't do) add up. Each new day brings with it little choices that will lead to big *good* things or big *bad* things.

A man going on a journey entrusted his property to his servants. To one he gave five talents of money, to another two talents, and to another one talent, each according to his ability. The man who had received the five talents went at once and put his money to work and gained five more. So also, the one with the two talents gained two more. But the man who had received the one talent went off, dug a hole in the ground, and hid his master's money. To the first two men, the master said, "Well done, good and faithful servant. You have been faithful with a few things; I will put you in charge of many things. Come and share your master's happiness!" But to the one who'd hidden his talent, he said, "You wicked, lazy servant! Take the talent from him and give it to the one who has the ten talents."

MATTHEW 25:14–28 PARAPHRASED

This parable of Jesus is a great example of "The Snowball Effect." Clearly, there are two paths:

- *The path to blessing* is marked with *discipline, consistency,* and *delayed gratification.* Those who walk this path begin with the end in mind. They have a clear picture of what they're shooting for, what they want to accomplish, what life will look like because of the decisions they're making. They're willing to wait for their reward, knowing they are doing the right things. When you choose this path, there are no shortcuts; consistent effort, sacrifice, and work are required. But this path will give them the strength to endure obstacles, hardship, challenges, and disappointment, to weather any storm, and to enjoy a peace that surpasses human understanding.
- *The path to breakdown* is marked with *laziness, compromise,* and *instant gratification.* Those who choose this path make excuses for not doing what they should. They aren't willing to sacrifice or do what's necessary for success, because the price is too high and it's too much work. When they don't see the results of their efforts, they give up all too easily. When you choose this path, you compromise your standards by letting your problems and poor decisions accumulate over time until they seem impossible to overcome. You sacrifice deep, long-term benefit for shallow, short-term pleasure.

Take a look around, and you'll see "The Snowball Effect" in motion every day. People suffer heart attacks because of small decisions to neglect their health over many years. Marriages suddenly fail, but it's the little things over the years that led to insurmountable problems. People survive great loss because of great faith and trust in God, cultivated by hours in the Word, in prayer, and in community. People of modest income retire with great wealth because they gave generously and saved wisely.

Every decision you make will accumulate like snow in a blizzard. So what path will you choose today?

Be a WisdomWalker!

Draw a line down the center of the page. Write "The Snowball Effect" at the top. On the left side, write "Path to Breakdown." List two or three things that you are doing (or not doing) that will lead to breakdown.

What consequences might you be experiencing as a result of your choices?

On the right side, write "Path to Blessing." List two or three things you are doing that will lead to blessing.

What other things could you do to change the course of your "Path to Breakdown" items?

A Step Deeper

Live Intentionally. Maximize Your Relationships. Pass the Torch.

Live It

1. Spend some time with God in prayer.
2. Ask God to help you think through your daily choices—whether they will lead to blessing or to breakdown.
3. Write down everything He tells you in the "My Insights" section.
4. Confess any wrongdoing and sinful behavior and ask Him to forgive you.
5. Ask Him to give you the courage and determination to change what needs to be changed.

Maximize It

1. Spend time with a trusted friend or mentor, going over these life areas:
   a. Do you save money each month, or spend more than you make?
   b. Do you invest quality and quantity time with God to build your character, or run out the door with a two-minute devotional or a quick "Thanks, God" at mealtimes?
   c. Do you invest in relationships, or are you too busy to make the effort?
   d. Do you care for your body with consistent exercise, good nutrition, and proper rest, or neglect your health?
2. Form an "action plan" for one of the areas. Take the first step today.

Pass It On

For additional study, read and reflect on:

- Proverbs 13:11; 14:15
- Luke 12:48

Share one of the above Scriptures with a friend or family member—and talk about how its wisdom and truth has influenced you to make some changes in your life.

My Insights

_____

_____

_____

_____

_____

Father, I know little things matter. Even the smallest things I do, think, and say add up over time. Nudge me to pay attention to the accumulation of my choices. Reveal what I need to change to get on the right path. Give me discipline to consistently do the work in the little things behind the scenes that will lead to life and big, good things. Help me sacrifice temporary pleasure for long-term satisfaction...for your glory!

20

JUST ONE WORD

WisdomWalks Principle
Narrow the focus for greater life change.

I'm only one person and I can't do everything.
But I can do something.
I will not let the fact that I can't do everything
prevent me from doing what I can.

HELEN KELLER

If you're like me, you've probably done your fair share of goal-setting at the start of each new year. Initially you're all fired up about the changes you're going to make. One month slides by, without much change happening, then another month. Before long, you begin to feel guilty as you fall short in your ambitious plans. *Why did I even try?* you wonder. And you give up.

Been there, done that. In fact, at one point, I was so frustrated with the whole process of New Year's Resolutions that I even tried boycotting the whole idea and avoided setting any goals at all. Needless to say, that didn't work, either. It just made me feel more guilty for being a slacker who didn't set any goals. No matter what I did, I wound up feeling defeated.

Then, over ten years ago, I started picking a one-word theme for the upcoming year. That's right. Just *one word*. Not a phrase, not a statement, just a single word. And since then, the principle has been nothing short of life-changing!

For me, this one-word exercise has become a focal point throughout the year. It helps bring clarity into a very complex world. The discipline of picking a one-word theme has stretched me in all areas—spiritually, physically and emotionally. God has transformed me in many ways through this exercise. I'm convinced that if you choose to try it, God will bring truth and revelation into your life, as well.

I do not consider myself yet to have taken hold of it. But one thing I do: Forgetting what is behind and straining toward what is ahead, I press on toward the goal to win the prize for which God has called me heavenward in Christ Jesus.

PHILIPPIANS 3:13–14

There's something else I want you to know. When you pick one word for the year, be careful. I'm serious. You know the phrase, "Be careful what you pray for"? Like when you pray for patience and all you get is trials, problems, and situations in which you need to practice patience? Well, the same goes for this. I guarantee that as soon as you pick the word, the battle will begin. So don't approach this exercise half-heartedly. You will get hammered, I promise. Satan will come after you full-force.

That's why this exercise isn't for people who want to pick a nice, comfortable word that will have no significant impact on their lives. It truly is a discipline for those who want to "press on toward the goal" and see God do great things in and through them. It's for those who want to live life to the fullest. No retreat. No regrets. Your goal should be to live out the adventure God has for you and to learn from the lessons along the way. This one-word exercise isn't a "to do" item on your list. Instead, it's a great journey of both victory and defeats—both of which are brought and laid at the feet of Christ.

So, if you want to grow more Christlike, pick a word. But be careful! It just might change the way you live.

Be a WisdomWalker!

Walk through the first four (see five and six under Maximize It) steps to developing a one-word theme:

1. Prepare your heart through prayer. What is God saying to you?

2. Search the Scriptures. What verses is the Lord bringing to your attention?

3. What area does God want to take hold of in your life and use for His glory?

4. Ask God for the word. Respond like Samuel, "Speak, Lord, your servant is listening." What is the Lord saying to you?

A Step Deeper

Live Intentionally. Maximize Your Relationships. Pass the Torch.

Live It

1. Spend some time with God in prayer.
2. Ask God to reveal to you the one word He wants you to pursue this year.
3. Write down everything He tells you in the "My Insights" section.
4. Confess any wrongdoing and sinful behavior and ask Him to forgive you.
5. Ask Him to give you the courage and determination to change what needs to be changed.

Maximize It

1. Talk to a trusted person about the one word the Lord has given you (step five) and why you believe this one word, in particular, is so important to you.

2. Brainstorm ways you can live out your word in your everyday life (step six).
3. Ask your mentor to check in with you on a regular basis to see how you're doing in following your good intentions through.

Pass It On

For additional study, read and reflect on:

- Mark 10:21
- Luke 10:42; 18:22
- John 9:25

Share one of the above Scriptures with a friend or family member— and talk about how its wisdom and truth has influenced you to make some changes in your life.

My Insights

_____

_____

_____

_____

_____

_____

_____

Lord, I ask that You will make this year a life-changing year. I want to live for You alone. Reveal Yourself to me as You show me what my one-word theme will be. Fill me with Your Holy Spirit. I realize that it is a journey of learning, not a task to accomplish. Through this process, I desire to know You better. Strengthen me as I live out my one word every day.

21

NO DOUBT!

WisdomWalks Principle
Take every thought captive.

*Where success is concerned, people are not measured
by inches, or pounds, or college degrees, or family background;
they are measured by the size of their thinking.*

DAVID J. SCHWARTZ

Have you ever struggled with self-doubt? I sure do. In fact, I constantly struggle with my thoughts of doubt, confusion, and pride, to name a few. I wrestle with doubting my ability and potential in a host of areas—including in my leadership at home and at work and in the arena of athletics, even though I'm no longer playing in the professional leagues. *Will people accept me as a teammate?* I wonder. *Will they want to follow my leadership? Am I a good leader? A good father? A good husband? Am I listening to the voices I should listen to—most of all, Your voice, God?*

But usually it's my *mind* that's my greatest challenge, not my physical or intellectual or social or relational abilities. Here's what I mean.

When I was in college, my lacrosse coach would post his daily practice plan before practice began. I'd speed over to it as soon as it was posted, because where my name was placed on the practice plan made all the difference in the world to me. You see, to me, where my coach placed my name on the list was the benchmark of my abilities. If he'd moved me a bit higher up the roster, I'd smile and think, *Hey, I must be doing pretty good.* If he moved me a bit lower down the roster, I'd sigh and think, *Hey, I better get it together and do better next time.*

Later I found that, to my great chagrin, that the coach had no real reason for moving the names around—he just moved them around! All that angst on my part and the wild speculation was for nothing…well, except for shooting up my blood pressure and stress. But in the long-term, that experience taught me a key principle that's now a part of my life: *no doubt!*

It's amazing what you can accomplish when you don't doubt the abilities God has given you.

WisdomWalking

We demolish arguments and every high-minded thing that is raised up against the knowledge of God, taking every thought captive to the obedience of Christ.

2 CORINTHIANS 10:4–5 HCSB

The apostle Paul was a pretty smart guy. "Take every thought captive," he said. In other words, don't let doubts get in your way. Confront them, get them out of the way, realize them as lies (pretensions) from the enemy, and plow through them. He even went further than that. "Demolish" them, he said. Now that's an active word meaning, "completely destroy them. Smash them flat so they'll never rise again."

If you abbreviate the concept "every thought captive," you get "etc." When I struggle with doubts, I remind myself of "etc." Then I surrender every thought and make it obedient to Christ.

Confronting doubt is still one of my toughest challenges as a Christian. It's a daily battle not to let my mind run with incorrect thoughts, with doubts of my abilities that God has granted me. But as I submit every stray thought to the Lord, more and more I'm keeping myself focused on what I need to do for the kingdom of Christ instead of letting my doubts sidetrack me.

What about you? Do you let doubts assail you? Discourage you? Keep you from doing what Christ wants you to accomplish?

Don't let others control your mind—only Christ has that privilege.

Be a WisdomWalker!

What kind of thoughts do you battle on a daily basis?

Why is it important to take every thought captive?

How could you apply the "etc." principle to your life?

A Step Deeper

Live Intentionally. Maximize Your Relationships. Pass the Torch.

Live It

1. Spend some time with God in prayer.
2. Ask God to reveal to you doubts that are holding you captive.
3. Write down everything He tells you in the "My Insights" section.
4. Confess any wrongdoing and sinful behavior and ask Him to forgive you.
5. Ask Him to give you the courage and determination to change what needs to be changed.

Maximize It

1. Ask a trusted friend this question: What things do you think I struggle with? Why do you think that? Is there something in my life that reveals I doubt myself and my abilities in that area?

2. Share with that person an area where you doubt yourself. Brainstorm some ways you could remind yourself, when in doubt, of the "etc." principle.
3. Pray together, asking God to help you learn to surrender every thought to Him.

Pass It On
For additional study, read and reflect on:

- Colossians 3:1–4

Share one of the above Scriptures with a friend or family member—and talk about how its wisdom and truth has influenced you to make some changes in your life.

My Insights

_____

_____

_____

_____

_____

_____

_____

_____

_____

_____

Lord, I need Your help. My thoughts often plague me. Free me from thoughts of doubt and pride—these I know are not of You. I desire to take every thought captive and surrender it to you. Let Your thoughts be my thoughts. In Your name I pray. Amen.

22

70 X 7

WisdomWalks Principle
Forgive...then forgive again.

Forgiveness is an act of the will, and the will can function regardless of the temperature of the heart.

CORRIE TEN BOOM

It's tough to forgive, isn't it? For one thing, it requires humility—something most of us aren't very good at. And second, it requires letting go of punishing the other person—or yourself, if you were the one in the wrong. Most of us like being in control, even if that control is hurting us and our relationships.

When the pain you've experienced is still fresh, forgiveness can be extremely difficult. But don't fall for the lie that if you hold on to the bitterness and grudges, the other person will be punished. The truth is, when you withhold forgiveness, everybody loses. You experience the destructive emotions of bitterness, anger, and resentment, and your relationship remains divided. If that condition lasts for too long, the relationship could be destroyed.

It's hard enough to extend forgiveness to someone who has wronged you, and harder still to ask God for forgiveness when you've messed up. But what's most difficult for me is asking someone *I* have wronged to forgive me, because it means expressing my failure, my sin, and accepting responsibility for what I've said or done to another person.

Interestingly, it's hardest for me to ask the person most important to me—my wife—for forgiveness. Is it like that for you, too? However, when I take full responsibility, offer no excuses, and don't try to shift any of the blame on her, our relationship is not only restored, but better for it. And you know what? When I'm humble and I ask for forgiveness, a strange thing happens: it encourages her to do the same in return!

Then Peter came to Jesus and asked, "Lord, how many times shall I forgive my brother when he sins against me? Up to seven times?" Jesus answered, "I tell you, not seven times, but seventy times seven."

MATTHEW 18:21–22

Don't you just love Peter? This impulsive guy thought he was being gracious. After all, forgiving someone seven times was a huge improvement over what the rabbis of the day taught; they only required three times. So Jesus' response of 70 x 7 must have rocked poor Peter's world, especially since the term that Jesus used actually meant "countless." Jesus was saying that love and forgiveness have no limits.

Then Jesus went on to tell a story about a king and a man who owed him ten thousand talents—a huge amount of money. The man begged for mercy, and the king graciously canceled his debts. You would think that receiving such forgiveness would have changed the man. But not so. That man did something all too human. When another servant owed that man a small amount of money and couldn't repay the debt, the man had the servant thrown into prison. The king heard about the man's lack of mercy and was furious. He confronted the man, saying, "I cancelled all that debt of yours. Shouldn't you have had mercy on your fellow servant just as I had on you?" So the king threw the man in jail.

We all need God's help with limitless forgiveness. The size of our sin debt that was canceled at the cross of Calvary should make us marvel. It's a gift that should motivate each of us to pass on the same measure of forgiveness to others. God's forgiveness is limitless. Shouldn't ours be, as well?

Be a WisdomWalker!

Are you the type of person who holds onto an offense or willingly forgives? Why? Give an example.

Think back to the last time you offended someone. Were you quick to ask for forgiveness, or did you avoid it like the plague?

Is it easier for you to forgive yourself, to forgive others, or to ask for God's forgiveness? Explain.

A Step Deeper

Live Intentionally. Maximize Your Relationships. Pass the Torch.

Live It

1. Spend some time with God in prayer.
2. Ask God to reveal to you any specific situations where you sinned against another person and also any specific situations where you are holding on to unforgiveness.
3. Write down everything He tells you in the "My Insights" section.
4. Confess any wrongdoing and sinful behavior and ask Him to forgive you.
5. Ask Him to give you the courage and determination to change what needs to be changed.

Maximize It

1. Ask a trusted friend to help you work through the specific situation(s) where you sinned against another person. Then, together, ask God to give you an opportunity to ask that person for forgiveness. Brainstorm ways you can be intentional about following through to make this happen.
2. Talk with your friend about any unforgiveness you are holding on to. How can you let that bitterness, anger, and frustration go? How can you

extend forgiveness and experience His healing and relief from all your negative emotions?

Pass It On
For additional study, read and reflect on:

- Genesis 4:24
- Matthew 6:9-15; 18:23-35
- Acts 10:43
- Ephesians 4:30–32
- 1 John 1:9

Share one of the above Scriptures with a friend or family member—and talk about how its wisdom and truth has influenced you to make some changes in your life.

My Insights

_____

_____

_____

_____

_____

_____

Father, Your forgiveness is limitless. You paid the price for my sin and canceled a debt that I could never repay. I am humbled and thankful. Help me to remember that truth when I have the opportunity to forgive others who have wronged me. Don't let me hang on to anger, resentment, and bitterness when forgiveness brings healing, freedom, and restoration. Put an unlimited amount of forgiveness in my heart and the humility to both ask for it and give it freely. Amen.

23

CAN YOU STAND THE HEAT?

WisdomWalks Principle
**Expect it, get ready for it,
and stand against it.**

One person with courage is a majority.
JIMMY PAGE

Can you remember exactly where you were when you heard that the Twin Towers were struck by planes flown by terrorists? The images from 9/11/2001 are still vividly entrenched in my mind. Although the photos from the sites were difficult to see, most of us remained glued to the television for days.

But without question, what sticks out most in my memory is the video footage of heroic police officers and firefighters running *toward* the Towers as thousands ran *away* in fear. In the face of terror and chaos, those men and women ran into the building on a mission to save lives. What incredible heroes!

The apostle Paul was like an old-time firefighter. He expected to face danger and hardship everywhere he went. He went into "burning buildings" on a mission to save lives. And since he expected to feel "the heat," he was ready for it, he endured it, and he took his stand against it. Are you?

WisdomWalking

And now, compelled by the Spirit, I am going to Jerusalem, not knowing what will happen to me there. I only know that in every city the Holy Spirit warns me that prison and hardships are facing me. However, I consider my life worth nothing to me, if only I may finish the

*race and complete the task the Lord Jesus has given me—the task of
testifying to the gospel of God's grace.*

ACTS 20:22–24

Life is full of challenges and obstacles. The Holy Spirit even warned Paul
about them. Jesus says to expect tough times but also encourages us to be
courageous in the face of adversity and to trust Him.

The easy road is for passive people. The rocky road is for those who want
more than personal happiness, accumulation of stuff, and then retirement.

God continually calls us to engage the enemy, our own sinful desires,
the culture, injustice, poverty, and evil. In Ephesians 6:10–20, Paul reveals
that the real battle happens in the spiritual realm; and if we rely on our own
strength and talent, we will be defeated. Our fight isn't really against other
people. We have an enemy who will do everything he can to steal, kill, and
destroy. If he can discourage you, he will. If he can divide us, he will. If he
can cause doubt and disbelief, he will.

The battle is won or lost by those who rely on the power of God and who:

Expect it. Jesus says, "In this world you will have trouble. But take heart!
I have overcome the world" (John 16:33). Better still, He promises peace
right in the middle of the battle.

Get ready for it. And stand against it.

The only way to prepare for and stand up to a spiritual battle is to put on
spiritual armor as you enter each day:

Be true. The Belt of Truth: This belt holds together all the other parts of
the armor. When you practice integrity and have a clear conscience, you
can have no fear. You never have to look over your shoulder or wonder
when a lie will catch up to you. Jesus is the truth, so by studying His life and
asking Him to guide you, you'll know the right thing to do.

Be right. The Breastplate of Righteousness: True righteousness only comes
when your heart is made right by faith in Christ. His forgiveness is forever. But
asking for forgiveness for your sin each day keeps this protection in place.

Be ready. The Shoes of the Gospel: When you wear these shoes, it means
you are ready to share your faith in Christ. You seek opportunities to live
out your faith and show others the love of Jesus. And you're not afraid to
walk into the tough situations or to take a stand for your faith.

Be sure. The Shield of Faith. The shield was typically large (four feet by two feet) and could be interlocked with the shields of other soldiers to form a nearly impenetrable barrier. Faith protects you from the fiery darts of the Devil. He tells lies, appeals to your sinful desires, and wants you to doubt God's faithfulness—all with the goal of getting you to disobey God. But faith is being sure of what you hope for and certain of what you can't yet see. It is complete trust in Christ.

Be smart. The Helmet of Salvation. The helmet protects your mind and the way you think. You need to continually renew your mind if you want to have a transformed life (Romans 12:1–2). When you get to know His Word and put it into practice, you are unlikely to fall into negativity, pessimism, criticism, and complaint. A positive attitude rooted in His truth and the assurance of eternal life brings peace in the midst of the storm.

Be skilled. The Sword of the Spirit. When you know the Word of God, He brings verses to mind right when you need them most. Then you can't be led away by false teaching. Jesus used God's Word to address the attacks and temptations of the Devil in the wilderness, and you can do the same.

Like the firefighters on 9/11, you are called to rescue. Do you expect the heat? Are you ready for it? And will you stand against it?

Be a WisdomWalker!

What armor from the above list do you feel you have firmly in place? Describe why.

Which part of the armor leaves you vulnerable to attack? Why?

A Step Deeper

Live Intentionally. Maximize Your Relationships. Pass the Torch.

Live It

1. Spend some time with God in prayer.

2. Ask God to reveal to you where the weak spots in your armor are.
3. Write down everything He tells you in the "My Insights" section.
4. Confess any wrongdoing and sinful behavior and ask Him to forgive you.
5. Ask Him to give you the courage and determination to change what needs to be changed.

Maximize It

1. Brainstorm with a trusted friend what three things you could do to put on the full armor of God each day.
2. How would putting on this armor help prepare you for everyday life?

Pass It On

For additional study, read and reflect on:

- Matthew 7:24–27
- Ephesians 6:10–20
- 1 Peter 3:15

Share one of the above Scriptures with a friend or family member—and talk about how its wisdom and truth has influenced you to make some changes in your life.

My Insights

_____

_____

_____

_____

Father, I know that I must be prepared always to face a spiritual enemy who wants to bring doubt, division, and discouragement. And the only way to be ready for life is to put on Your armor. Lord, help me put on each piece at the start of the day so I can take my stand and enjoy Your peace.

24

LIFE DETOX

WisdomWalks Principle
Put off the old; put on the new.

de·tox·i·fy (dē'täksə‚fī) verb
[1] To remove, counteract, or destroy the toxic
 properties of something poisonous.
[2] To set someone free from a harmful dependence
 or addiction.

One of the most popular "movements" in the health and fitness world is the concept of a "Detox Diet." You can hardly pick up a magazine without some reference to detoxifying your body. The idea of removing the accumulation of harmful substances from the food you eat, the stress you feel, and environmental toxins is beneficial.

In fact, eating a super-clean diet and taking proper supplements for a ten- to forty-day period can restore a healthy internal environment and promote good health. You'll most likely experience increased energy, reduced aches and pains, better digestion, and fewer illnesses. Capturing and removing toxic substances and replacing them with healthy things are solid life practices.

They don't happen automatically without being intentional.

WisdomWalking

Since we have these promises, dear friends, let us purify ourselves from everything that contaminates body and spirit, perfecting holiness out of reverence for God.

2 CORINTHIANS 7:1

The Bible gives plenty of instruction for detoxifying your life. In this verse, the apostle Paul hits it hard: "purify ourselves from *everything* that contaminates body and spirit." Purifying the body includes paying attention to what we eat and drink, staying away from harmful things like smoking or drugs, getting proper exercise and enough rest, and not engaging in immoral sexual behavior. Purifying the Spirit includes our words, thoughts, attitudes, actions, and desires.

Clearly, detoxification is not a passive process. We have to act. We put filters on our computers to block viruses, filters on home heating systems to remove dust and allergens, and oil filters on cars to remove the junk so the car performs and lasts. But we often don't do much to protect our body, our mind, or our heart.

"Life Detox" involves three parts:

Identify. Each of us has harmful stuff in our life that causes damage. The first step is to identify it, then capture it—just as your liver is designed to identify harmful substances, capture the toxic material, and remove it from your body so it doesn't cause illness. Toxic material can enter your system in a number of ways: through movies, TV programs, Internet sites with inappropriate or offensive material, or music with a great beat but a destructive message. Unhealthy food could destroy health over time. Other harmful stuff is dwelling on the negative, having a pattern of critical words, or getting frustrated and angry easily. No matter what the toxic material, you've got to see it for what it is first.

Remove. Once we know the harmful things we're exposing ourselves to we can remove them. Some things just need to go—like a cancerous tumor needs to be removed. Colossians 3 says to remove whatever hinders us from living a life that pleases God. The short list includes anger, slander, foul language, lust, greed, jealousy, lies, and more. These things poison us; we've got to root them out and get rid of them. In Proverbs 4:23–27 says to guard our heart, hold our tongue, keep our eyes from viewing garbage, and take the narrow road of obedience. Removing toxic behavior requires you to put up guardrails, draw hard lines you won't cross, and get rid of everything that causes you to stumble or fail. You must remove yourself from compromising situations and reduce the opportunity for sin.

Replace. It's one thing to stop doing hurtful things—to remove temptations and put up boundaries. But living a holy life requires us to replace the bad with good, and replace the "don'ts" with "dos." Matthew 12:43–45 reveals what happens when we try to clean up all the bad things and neglect to replace them with good. It's like trying to give up sweets without replacing them with a healthy alternative, or trying to quit smoking without replacing it with a habit. Eventually the bad habits return with a vengeance! It's time to put off the "old" and put on the "new." Wrong thinking must be replaced with right thinking (the positive, the possible, and the pure). Criticism must be replaced with encouragement. Anger must be replaced with love and tenderness.

A Life Detox is a perfect way to purify yourself from everything that contaminates you—mind, body, and spirit.

Be a WisdomWalker!

Divide a page into three columns with *Body, Mind, Spirit* headings. List two or three items in each category that might be contaminating your life.

Circle the most toxic item from each list. Why is it so harmful in your life?

What one healthy habit could replace each toxic behavior you circled?

A Step Deeper

Live Intentionally. Maximize Your Relationships. Pass the Torch.

Live It

1. Spend some time with God in prayer.
2. Ask God to reveal to you any toxic behaviors that you're not already aware of.
3. Write down everything He tells you in the "My Insights" section.
4. Confess any wrongdoing and sinful behavior and ask Him to forgive you.
5. Ask Him to give you the courage and determination to change what needs to be changed.

Maximize It

1. Share one item from your "toxic behavior" list with a trusted friend or mentor. How does this one item influence yours—and others'—lives?
2. Brainstorm together how you could actively and intentionally replace the toxic behavior with a healthy habit.
3. Ask your friend to check in with you on a daily basis for the next five days to encourage you in this healthy habit.

Pass It On

For additional study, read and reflect on:

- Psalm 19:13
- Matthew 12:43–45
- Romans 8:1–14
- 2 Corinthians 7:1
- Colossians 3:1–17

Share one of the above Scriptures with a friend or family member—and talk about how its wisdom and truth has influenced you to make some changes in your life.

My Insights

_____

_____

_____

_____

Father, I know it's time to take action and purify my life from everything that contaminates me. I also know it's time to pursue a holy life out of reverence for You. I want my life to be different. Please help me to make decisions that lead to life. Cleanse me of my sin and set me free from its burden. Help me find specific ways to replace the old with the new and to walk in good health—mind, body, and spirit.

25

A GAME-CHANGING MOMENT

WisdomWalks Principle
Be sold out for what you believe.

Faith is a living and unshakeable confidence.
A belief in God so assured that a man
would die a thousand deaths for its sake.

MARTIN LUTHER

Everyone has at least one favorite game-changing sports moment. It's that one play during a game that changes everything. In a single moment, momentum shifts, and it alters the outcome of the game. Sometimes, the play not only changes the game, but also an athlete's entire career. Some of my personal favorite game-changers include David Tyree's catch from Eli Manning on fourth and long in the 2008 Super Bowl, Christian Laettner's last-second jumper in the 1992 NCAA Tournament, Kirk Gibson's 1988 pinch-hit HR in the World Series, and, of course, Doug Flutie's famous "Hail Mary" pass in 1984.

Game-changers have a huge impact on sports history. Some would say those moments are why we watch and play sports. But the real question is not what sports game-changers are the most impacting, but rather, what spiritual game-changer has most impacted your life? Do you have one of those moments—one that altered everything in your life and forced you to see life differently?

The ultimate game-changer for anyone is the moment you place your faith and trust in Jesus. If you have done that already, what will be your next spiritual game-changer? Has God ever gripped your life in such a way that shifted the spiritual momentum and changed the way you see things?

But everything that was a gain to me, I have considered to be a loss because of Christ.

PHILIPPIANS 3:7 HCSB

For me, the ultimate game-changer happened on August 4, 2007. I was standing in front of a grave in Seoul, South Korea. It was the burial site of someone I didn't even know. I was in Korea with an FCA ministry team doing a sports camp during the 100-year anniversary of the Pyongyang Great Revival. In 1907, God had stirred in the hearts of men and women in Korea to be authentic—to come clean before others. It started with the leaders going before their congregations to lay down their pride and admit their sins. But it had started even before that, with the many early missionaries to Korea, who were beheaded, speared, and burned. Their blood was the catalyst that brought massive revival.

Visiting 510 graves at the Foreigners Cemetery Park in Seoul that honored the first Christian martyrs in Korea was a spiritual gut-check. As I walked through the grave sites and saw the quotes and Scriptures on the graves, I was overwhelmed. But the one that altered everything for me was the tombstone of a woman named Ruby Kendrick. She was a young missionary from Texas who had responded to the call to preach the Gospel to the Korean people. She died at age twenty-four, only eight months after she arrived in Korea, and her death inspired other missionaries to take her place.

This was the quote on her tombstone: "If I had a thousand lives to give, Korea should have them all." Now, that is the true outworking of Philippians 3:7. Ruby Kendrick was totally surrendered to the Lord's work. She sacrificed everything, even her own life, for the sake of the call.

I thought, *If I had a thousand lives to give, who or what would deserve them all?* I couldn't shake that question. What was I so sold out for that I would offer up life after life for it? More importantly, what was I willing to do with this one life I have? The spiritual momentum of my heart shifted that day. God confirmed in me that if I had a thousand lives to give, athletes and coaches should get them all! I long to see the entire sports world transformed by God's love, and I ask the Lord every day to bring revival to the athletic community and say, "Lord, use me however You wish to help make that happen."

What Jesus wants from you is a desire to serve Him with reckless abandon. What are you sold out for? If you had a thousand lives, who or what would deserve them all?

Be a WisdomWalker!

What's your favorite sports game-changer? When you remember it, how does it make you feel?

Do you have a spiritual game-changing moment? What happened?

Since that time, what has happened in your life? Has there been significant change? Why or why not? If so, explain the change.

A Step Deeper

Live Intentionally. Maximize Your Relationships. Pass the Torch.

Live It

1. Spend some time with God in prayer.
2. Ask God to stir your heart with the answer to the question, "If I had a thousand lives to give, who or what would deserve them all?"
3. Write down everything He tells you in the "My Insights" section.
4. Confess any wrongdoing and sinful behavior and ask Him to forgive you.
5. Ask Him to give you the courage and determination to change what needs to be changed.

Maximize It

1. Talk with a trusted friend about your spiritual game-changer, if you have one. If not, talk about what you're discovering about your answer to the question, "If I had a thousand lives to give, who or what would deserve them all?"
2. If you could have any words engraved on your tombstone, what would they be? Why?
3. With your friend, ask God to bring revival into your hearts and lives.

Pass It On
For additional study, read and reflect on:

- Acts 9:1–19
- 2 Corinthians 4:16–18
- Philippians 3:7–11

Share one of the above Scriptures with a friend or family member—and talk about how its wisdom and truth has influenced you to make some changes in your life.

My Insights

_____

_____

_____

_____

_____

Lord, if I had a thousand lives to give, You would deserve them all. But what I struggle with is how to live that out. Who or what deserves a thousand of my lives? How should I offer my one life? Help me, Jesus, to see clearly how my life should be lived. Reveal Your desire for me. Thank You, Jesus, for touching my life and transforming it. In Your name I pray. Amen.

26

DOG ON A LEASH

WisdomWalks Principle
Life is a battleground, not a playground.

When the enemy seems close, Jesus is closer.
And He commands you to "fear not" 365 times in the Bible—
once for each new day.

ANNE ORTLUND

I love to get a run in every morning, no matter the conditions. But I've learned that if I don't do it early, it won't happen, especially when I'm traveling.

Several years ago, while in Korea for a camp, I found a good loop down some back streets and trails and began running in the dim light of the early morning. Then, out of nowhere, a dog charged at me.

I practically leaped out of my shoes as I jumped away from the attacking dog. Fortunately, the dog made it only to the edge of the street, then stopped.

For a moment, I wondered why he hadn't charged further; then I realized the dog was on a leash. That changed everything. I immediately calmed down and began to run again with confidence, chuckling to myself at my nervousness.

The next morning, I was ready. I approached the same spot with confidence. Sure enough, the exact same dog did what he was good at: charging hard with lots of bark. But this time, my perspective was completely different. It was just a dog on a leash. I respected the dog, but I did not fear the dog like I had before. Seeing the dog was on a leash made a huge difference in my response and attitude in the following days as I ran.

Therefore, submit to God. But resist the Devil, and he will flee from you.

JAMES 4:7 HCSB

It occurred to me recently that Satan is just like that dog. He is a dog on a leash. Unfortunately, many Christians respond to him like I did that first day with the dog. They never notice that God has him on a leash. They are surprised by Satan, and they fear and worry how he is attacking and impacting their lives.

Yes, Satan is real, just like the dog I encountered. It wasn't a tape recorder of a dog barking that scared me. It was a real, scary dog that wanted to maul me. If he hadn't been on a leash, I wouldn't be writing this WisdomWalk. And, just like that dog, but on a much larger scale, Satan wants to harm us and destroy us. John 10:10 reminds us that he will steal, kill, and destroy!

While we must recognize the power and evil of our spiritual opponent, we must keep him in perspective. When I ran the following days, I respected the dog, but I did not fear the dog. He had his boundaries, so I made sure I did not run on the side of the road that put me in his range. I ran with confidence, knowing he had limits, but I did not try to get as close as possible to provoke him. In the same way, we as Christians can't live our lives seeing how close we can get to Satan without getting bit. Instead of asking ourselves how close we can get to the line without sinning, we must ask how close we can get to the Lord.

Do you respect Satan's power and realize that he is gunning for you? If you are having an impact for Christ, you have a big bull's-eye on your chest. Satan doesn't want you to experience joy in your life. If he can't take you to hell because you are a disciple of Christ, he'll do everything in his power to make sure you don't draw others to Jesus.

So, how are you doing? Do you have a good understanding of Satan and how he tries to work in your life? Do you realize that Satan is a dog on a leash? Yes, respect his power, but do not fear him. If he gets you to live in fear, then you'll become ineffective as believers. Don't let Satan catch you by surprise. Jesus has already won the battle. Instead, focus on doing His work, His way.

Be a WisdomWalker!

In what three top ways is Satan gunning for you? Be specific about how he's trying to steal, kill, and destroy you.

When Satan's at work, are you surprised? Why or why not? What has affected your perspective?

A Step Deeper

Live Intentionally. Maximize Your Relationships. Pass the Torch.

Live It

1. Spend some time with God in prayer.
2. Ask God to reveal to you ways Satan is trying to work his way in your life.
3. Write down everything He tells you in the "My Insights" section.
4. Confess any wrongdoing and sinful behavior and ask Him to forgive you.
5. Ask Him to give you the courage and determination to change what needs to be changed.

Maximize It

1. What does it mean for you to respect Satan's influence, but not fear him? Talk about this with a trusted friend or mentor.

2. How can we, as Christians, fight from a position of victory? From the perspective that Christ has already won?

3. How could this altered perspective—that Satan is a dog on a leash—help you to be victorious against him in the coming week?

Pass It On

For additional study, read and reflect on:

- 2 Kings 6:15–19
- 2 Corinthians 10:3–5
- Ephesians 6:10–18

Share one of the above Scriptures with a friend or family member—and talk about how its wisdom and truth has influenced you to make some changes in your life.

My Insights

_____

_____

_____

_____

_____

_____

_____

_____

Jesus, thank You for Your victory. Give me Your eyes so I can correctly see the battle that rages in the spiritual realm. I know that, at times, I give Satan too much credit and other times not enough. Help me, Lord, to have the right perspective. Thank You, Jesus, for protecting me and already giving me victory because of what You did on the cross. In Your name I pray. Amen.

27

DREAM ON!

WisdomWalks Principle
Follow the visions God places on your heart.

Big dreams create the magic that stir men's souls to greatness.
BILL MCCARTNEY

When I was eight years old, I did a lot of dreaming. My dad would take me to watch college lacrosse games, and I would stand down by the field, trying to get as close as I could to the big, strong, fast athletes who were living out their dream. I would say over and over again, "One day I wish I could play on that field!"

Looking back, I realize the incredible power of dreams. My dream drove me for ten years until I finally had the opportunity to fulfill that dream. When I was eighteen years old, I stepped onto that exact same field to live my dream as a college lacrosse player. Not only did the ten-year-old dream come true, but I didn't know that God had a dream for me too, and it was much bigger than mine. I was dreaming just college lacrosse, but He was dreaming professional lacrosse. I was drafted in the first round by the Baltimore Thunder, and I continued my career for four years playing professional indoor lacrosse. God allowed me to use my gift of lacrosse to reach thousands for Him, because of a dream He had for me!

What dreams is God placing on your heart? Those dreams are indeed powerful. But what God wants to do with them is so much bigger than you can ever imagine.

WisdomWalking

Then Joseph had a dream. When he told it to his brothers, they hated him even more. He said to them, "Listen to this dream I had: There we were, binding sheaves of grain in the field. Suddenly my sheaf stood up, and your sheaves gathered around it and bowed down to my sheaf." "Are you really going to reign over us?" his brothers asked him. "Are you really going to rule us?" So they hated him even more because of his dream and what he had said.

GENESIS 37:5–8 HCSB

Joseph had a dream at age seventeen, but his dream was not fulfilled for more than twenty years! He stayed faithful to the vision God had given him, even though he was betrayed by his brother, sold into slavery, hauled to a distant land, and he spent thirteen years unjustly incarcerated in prison. But God's dream for Joseph was even bigger than his own. Joseph's dreams would impact an entire nation—and would save his own family from destruction.

From Joseph's experiences, here are Ten Principles of Dreaming that can encourage you as you dream big for Jesus:

1. Dreams come from God.
2. God-sized dreams stretch us.
3. Dreams ignite energy, passion, and drive.
4. People often make fun of dreamers.
5. There is always a season of preparation with dreams.
6. Dreams take time to be realized.
7. Be an encourager of other people's dreams.
8. Dreams are for all ages.
9. Don't miss the fulfillment of the dream when it comes true.
10. Dreams should glorify God, not us.

A lot of times, we think we can accomplish great things in life without the effort. We see the dream clearly, but instead of becoming a dream-doer, we settle for being a dreamer. The fulfillment of a dream requires vision and action. Bear Grylls of *Man vs. Wild* says it best: "Dreams are great, but they have a price. Dreams are made possible in those dark hours, the unsung hours behind the scenes. And if you want them, you have to pay that price."

Let the dream ignite your passion, but let your actions be the fuel that helps you convert the dream into reality.

So what are you dreaming of? Go ahead—dream big!

Be a WisdomWalker!

What big dreams do you have? Why are these important to you?

What dreams have you given up on? Why?

A Step Deeper

Live Intentionally. Maximize Your Relationships. Pass the Torch.

Live It

1. Spend some time with God in prayer.
2. Ask God to reveal dreams you have that He could use in a big way.
3. Write down everything He tells you in the "My Insights" section.
4. Confess any wrongdoing and sinful behavior and ask Him to forgive you.
5. Ask Him to give you the courage and determination to change what needs to be changed.

Maximize It

1. Share your big dreams with a trusted friend or mentor. Brainstorm together: how might God use those dreams?
2. Think of others you know who have dreams. Whose dreams might you encourage? How?

3. Ask God to work out your dreams in His way, in His timing.

Pass It On

For additional study, read and reflect on:

- Genesis 37
- Acts 2:17

Share one of the above Scriptures with a friend or family member—and talk about how its wisdom and truth has influenced you to make some changes in your life.

My Insights

_____

_____

_____

_____

_____

_____

_____

_____

_____

_____

_____

Lord, I know all dreams come from You. Continue to ignite the passion in my soul to dream the dreams that You alone have for me. Forgive me for giving up on dreams I have not seen fulfilled. Help me to press on and be faithful to the calling that You have placed on my heart and in my life.

28

DON'T GO IT ALONE

WisdomWalks Principle
Life is not a "me" thing—it's a "we" thing.

If you want to go fast—go alone.
If you want to go far—go together.
AFRICAN PROVERB

There's something in each of us that says, *I can stand alone. I don't need others. I can do life by myself, thank you very much.*

But is that really the truth? Being self-disciplined and independent is important, yes. But this comment I once heard from an athlete sums it up: "We would have a great team except for all my teammates." Yes, we all talk "team," but what do we value the most? Self.

The same thing happens in our spiritual lives. *Doesn't loving God come down to just me?* we wonder. Well, yes and no. Yes, we do need to love God with all *our* heart. But no, we can't do it alone. Isolation is our silent enemy. It's quite different from silence or solitude (two powerful spiritual disciplines). There's pride in isolation—thinking we can live our faith through our own power. As a result, we distance ourselves from those who know us best.

Isolation makes us believe we can commit sins...and be free of consequences. King David had that mindset until the prophet Nathan showed up and told him exactly how badly he was messing up (2 Samuel 12). Also, isolation convinces us that we're the only ones wrestling with a particular problem. We begin to believe no one will understand, so why open up and seek help? After all, if we just keep a lid on our problems, we'll contain them. But secretly they control us.

Don't fall into the trap of isolation. Living the Christian life is not a "me" thing—it's a "we" thing.

Iron sharpens iron, and one man sharpens another.

PROVERBS 27:17 HCSB

You won't find the word *accountability* in the Bible, but Christ and His disciples modeled it continually. The disciples were also sent out in pairs. Accountability is non-negotiable in the Christian life. For over twenty years, I've had an accountability partner—someone I meet with on a weekly basis who asks me tough questions. That accountability has allowed me to live for Christ with greater purity and passion because someone else is checking to make sure I'm doing what I've committed to do (i.e., spending time with God daily, keeping my eyes pure, spending quality and quantity time with my family, making wise financial decisions, and training my body). Every aspect of my life is evaluated on a weekly basis, and it keeps my mind, body, and soul on the right track. If you don't have someone like that in your life, it's time to find one. The sooner, the better.

I once heard that the banana that's separated from the bunch gets peeled first. That analogy hits home, doesn't it? Don't think you can live for Christ without being connected.

For accountability to work long term, you must have:

Transparency. You must be willing to be seen for who you really are. Many of us are afraid to let anyone see who we are deep down. We're afraid of rejection or of damaging our reputation so we put on the mask.

Choice. You cannot make someone commit to things they don't want to do. You are not the Holy Spirit, and you are not their conscience. Each person must willingly change.

Confidentiality. Everything shared goes no further than the two of you.

Commitment. Each of you must be willing to live to a higher standard and be held to the commitments you make. The person across the table must have a deep desire to see you succeed. Your shared goal is to help each other live your best for God.

Confrontation. Resist the temptation to "go easy" on each other because of your close friendship. Accountability requires confronting the reality of the situation—facing the truth—and accepting the challenge to do the right thing.

Compass. The Word of God must serve as the compass and the standard for all counsel, encouragement, and correction. Worldly wisdom without the application of the Word is useless.

Be a WisdomWalker!

Do you tend to live, act, and think as an isolated individual—or as part of a team? Explain your answer, using examples from your life.

How have others helped you in your spiritual journey? Do you have an accountability partner? Why or why not?

A Step Deeper

Live Intentionally. Maximize Your Relationships. Pass the Torch.

Live It

1. Spend some time with God in prayer.
2. Ask God to reveal any areas where you're living in isolation mode.
3. Write down everything He tells you in the "My Insights" section.
4. Confess any wrongdoing and sinful behavior and ask Him to forgive you.
5. Ask Him to give you the courage and determination to change what needs to be changed.

Maximize It

1. Discuss with a trusted friend or mentor why isolation is so easy and accountability is so hard.

2. Share honestly about an area of your life in which you act in isolation. What happens (or has happened) as a result?
3. Why is there power in confessing your sin and mistakes to another person? How can you take a step toward accountability today?

Pass It On
For additional study, read and reflect on:

- Romans 15:1–2
- Ephesians 4:25
- Hebrews 3:13
- James 5:16

Share one of the above Scriptures with a friend or family member—and talk about how its wisdom and truth has influenced you to make some changes in your life.

My Insights

_____

_____

_____

_____

_____

_____

_____

Jesus, I want to finish the race of faith well. I don't want to drop out or even stumble across the finish line. Help me to find friends who can help me finish strong, and whom I can help as well. I ask for strength to break the sin of isolation and secrecy. Help me to be open and transparent with at least one other believer. I do not want to live out my faith alone anymore. In Your name I pray. Amen.

29

THE 10-CAMEL DEAL

WisdomWalks Principle
Serve big, or go home!

Everybody can be great...because anybody can serve.
You don't have to have a college degree to serve.
You don't have to make your subject and verb agree to serve.
You only need a heart full of grace. A soul generated by love.

MARTIN LUTHER KING JR.

I don't know about you, but I find it more and more difficult to get really good service. And it's not just that people aren't very helpful anymore. They also tend to have a "you're bothering me" attitude to go along with it. Strange, isn't it, when helping you is part of their job description?

But I've also noticed that *I* can get frustrated even at little things, like having to wait in a long line at the grocery store—especially when there's only one cashier working, with three or four more standing around watching and chatting. And don't you just love it when they open up a new line and the people at the back hustle over to get to the front? Or how about when someone beats you to the "express lane" and they have a cart full of twenty-nine items (way over the twelve-item limit!)! It drives me nuts!

Being a "servant" isn't usually the first thing that pops to the forefront of my human nature. But it's the very kind of person that God is shaping me...and you...to become.

WisdomWalking

The servant took ten of his master's camels and took with him all kinds of good things from his master. He set out for Aram Naharaim and the town of Nahor. He had the camels kneel down near the well outside the town at the time the women draw water. "May it be that when I say to a girl, 'Please let down your jar that I may have a drink,' and she says, 'Drink, and I'll water your camels too,' let her be the one you have chosen for your servant Isaac." Before he had finished praying, Rebekah came out with her jar on her shoulder. She went down to the spring, filled her jar, and came up again. The servant hurried to meet her and said, "Please give me a little water from your jar." After she had given him a drink, she said, "I'll draw water for your camels too, until they have finished drinking." So she quickly emptied her jar into the trough, ran back to the well to draw more water, and drew enough for all his camels.

GENESIS 24:10–20 PARAPHRASED

I am greatly convicted of my selfishness and laziness each time I read the story of Rebekah in Genesis 24. The backstory? Abraham had sent one of his devoted servants to find a wife for his son Isaac. When the servant got to his destination, they rested near the well. When Rebekah came to the well, he asked her for water and she gladly served him.

But what she offered next was remarkable—she offered to get water for his ten camels! At first glance, you might be tempted to say, "That's no big deal. So she got water for his camels." But the ante is upped when you realize that she had to draw the water by hand from the well, then carry it to where the camels were. Each camel, depending on the heat of the season, the weight of the cargo, and how long they'd gone without water, could drink between five and twenty-five gallons of water—and Rebekah had no way of knowing. She would have to get between fifty and 250 gallons of water from the well; that's between 400 and 2,000 pounds!

This story is one of the greatest illustrations of a servant's heart I've ever read. Rebekah was *kind and humble*; she *responded* to the needs of the man, *anticipated* the needs of the camels, *moved* quickly, *sacrificed* to help others, *exceeded* expectations, and had a *pure motive*. Can you imagine if everybody today was like Rebekah? What if you and I were like her?

Serving always starts with humility. Servants look for ways to anticipate and respond to the needs of others, even when that requires personal sacrifice and hard work. Servants go above and beyond, especially when they have nothing to gain. That's what "Ten-Camel" service is all about. And that's exactly the life Jesus lived—one of service and sacrifice. Talk about going above and beyond—He laid down His very life for me and for you!

When you're a "Ten-Camel" server, everyone will want to know why you're doing what you're doing. Serving gives you incredible opportunities to show the love of Jesus. So what are you waiting for?

Be a WisdomWalker!

The last time you went out to a restaurant was your server pleasant and helpful? Did he or she anticipate your needs and offer pleasant, helpful suggestions? Or did you walk away thinking you'd never go back because of that server's attitude? Tell the story.

Now think about your actions at that same restaurant. Did you think about ways to encourage your server, or were you all about you? Explain.

Are you a "Ten-Camel" servant? Would your friends and colleagues identify you that way? Why or why not?

A Step Deeper

Live Intentionally. Maximize Your Relationships. Pass the Torch.

Live It

1. Spend some time with God in prayer.
2. Ask God to reveal to you how you might serve others.
3. Write down everything He tells you in the "My Insights" section.

4. Confess any wrongdoing and sinful behavior and ask Him to forgive you.
5. Ask Him to give you the courage and determination to change what needs to be changed.

Maximize It

1. Discuss how you could intentionally serve in a "Ten-Camel" way. Could you do something unexpected at home, school, work, or in your community?
2. Make the focus of your next restaurant meal to intentionally serve your server. How could you encourage and compliment that server?
3. In what way could you serve beyond your own—and others'—wildest expectations this week? How might you point others to Jesus?

Pass It On

For additional study, read and reflect on:

- Matthew 5:40–42; 20:28
- Mark 9:35
- Philippians 1:1; 2:1–4

Share one of the above Scriptures with a friend or family member—and talk about how its wisdom and truth has influenced you to make some changes in your life.

My Insights

_____

_____

_____

_____

Father, on this day, I choose to intentionally serve others. Help me to find extraordinary ways to do just that every day. Give me humility to consider others' needs as more important than my own so that Your love shines through me. Help me to follow in the footsteps of Jesus, who came to earth to serve others in an extraordinary way.

30

GLORY HOUND?

WisdomWalks Principle
Don't steal the glory.

God is not interested in receiving secondhand glory from our activity.
God receives glory from His activity through our lives.

HENRY T. BLACKABY

Most cars don't even travel 422.6 miles in three days. But Gary Brasher did the unthinkable: three iron-distance triathlons in three consecutive days, for a total of 422.6 miles! I've run a few marathons in my life, but those aren't anything, compared to what Gary has accomplished.

I was privileged to be with Gary for a few days while he was grinding out part of his crazy training schedule. One morning, I was heading out for a six-mile run, and he was working on his daily six *hours* of training. Talk about being on a whole different level.

After spending my whole life around athletes, I know one thing for sure. There's always a bit of "glory hound" in competitors. We compete to impress others and get recognition. If anyone could be justified in walking around with his chest poked out, it would be Gary. But one of the awesome things I discovered about Gary, as I spent time with him, is that he is *not* a glory hound. In fact, he's an entirely opposite breed. He wasn't doing 422.6 miles for himself. He was doing it for the Lord.

WisdomWalking

When all our enemies heard this, all the surrounding nations were intimidated and lost their confidence, for they realized that this task had been accomplished by our God.

NEHEMIAH 6:16 HCSB

If anyone in the Bible could have been justified in being a glory hound, it would have been the great leader Nehemiah. After all, he rebuilt a huge wall in fifty-two days—an unbelievable accomplishment. He did the unthinkable, even though everyone told him he wouldn't succeed. But Nehemiah 6:16 makes it crystal clear how he did it—or *didn't* do it at all. This incredible task was accomplished by God, not Nehemiah. Nehemiah was smart and godly enough to give God the credit He was due. And therein lies the secret of greatness: "God did it. Not me."

That's a hard phrase to say sometimes, isn't it? Our classic response, when things go well, is usually, "Yeah, I did it…but I want to give God credit." But for Gary Brasher and for Nehemiah, it wasn't about giving God credit. It was about their desire to let everyone know that God accomplished those particular tasks from start to finish. They weren't doing things to make themselves look great, but to glorify God and give Him the credit. That makes both Gary and Nehemiah reflectors of God's glory.

In order to be a reflector of God's glory, we must be humble. Part of the reason most people look like glory hounds is because they don't know how to express humility. Humility isn't thinking less of yourself. It's thinking of yourself less. When we're preoccupied by thoughts of ourselves, our reputations and achievements, we have a hard time even recognizing that it's God who gave us the talents, skills, and gifts in the first place. That's why God reminds us in Deuteronomy to never forget that any success we may have is really just a gift from Him. He gave us the ability. Period. We can't take the credit!

The enemy has two sneaky strategies: to make us think we're Somebody, or to make us think we're Nobody. He wants to puff us up with pride so we grab the glory, or smack us down with shame so we never do anything big. Either way, he wins.

We may never do a triple-iron triathlon. We may never accomplish a huge task like building the wall of a city in fifty-two days. But each day we *are* doing something significant: we are representing Christ. So we must ask ourselves: *Am I a glory hound, or a glory reflector?*

It's simple. It's either "God did it," or "I did it." Which route will you choose?

Be a WisdomWalker!

Do you tend to be a glory hound, or a glory reflector? Why? What's the difference between saying, "God did it," and "I did it"?

If you were going to live the philosophy that "God did it all," how would your thoughts and actions change?

A Step Deeper

Live Intentionally. Maximize Your Relationships. Pass the Torch.

Live It

1. Spend some time with God in prayer.
2. Ask God to transform your perspective from glory hound to glory reflector.
3. Write down everything He tells you in the "My Insights" section.
4. Confess any wrongdoing and sinful behavior and ask Him to forgive you.
5. Ask Him to give you the courage and determination to change what needs to be changed.

Maximize It

1. Ask a trusted friend, "Do you see me as a person who wants the credit myself, or someone who is willing to give others and God the credit? Why?"
2. Is there a difference between the way you see yourself, and the way your friend sees you? If so, discuss the discrepancy and why it might exist.

3. Whom do you know who is a great example of a glory reflector? What can you learn from his or her example?

Pass It On

For additional study, read and reflect on:

- Zechariah 4:6
- Matthew 5:16
- John 15:8
- 1 Corinthians 10:31
- 1 Peter 4:11

Share one of the above Scriptures with a friend or family member—and talk about how its wisdom and truth has influenced you to make some changes in your life.

My Insights

_____

_____

_____

_____

_____

_____

Father, You and only You deserve the credit for anything I accomplish. Help me to identify those areas where I am a glory hound. Change my perspective so I will always be saying, "I didn't do it. God did it." More than anything in life, Lord, I want to be a glory reflector so that others won't see me, but Jesus. Amen.

31

PRAY IT UP!

WisdomWalks Principle
Pray like your life depends on it.

Pray like it all depends on God;
work like it all depends on you.

JOHN WESLEY

I can actually remember the day when there was no such thing as a cell phone. No texting. No IM. Seriously! And Moms everywhere made their kids carry a quarter in case they needed to make an emergency call from a pay phone. Communication was challenging then (especially if you lost the quarter from your pocket), but today it's instantaneous. In the click of a "Send" button, you can e-mail hundreds of friends and colleagues all across the world. You can be at a family barbecue and be texting your boss the answer to his urgent questions. Amazing, isn't it? I wonder where communication will be five years from now....

If communicating with each other is so easy and immediate (and important), why is it so tough to communicate with God? The statistics say that the average Christian prays about three minutes each day. That's about the same amount of time that I spend brushing my teeth, drying my hair, making my coffee, and a whole bunch of other things in my normal routine. Yet praying is communicating with my Creator—the Lord of the entire universe. That ought to give us pause—for a whole lot more than three minutes—shouldn't it?

WisdomWalking

This, then, is how you should pray: "Our Father in heaven, hallowed be thy name, your kingdom come, your will be done on earth as it is in heaven. Give us today our daily bread. Forgive us our debts, as we also have forgiven our debtors. And lead us not into temptation, but deliver us from the evil one."

MATTHEW 6:9-13

The disciples saw Jesus pray all the time. He would regularly get away to a quiet place to talk with His Father. They also witnessed power flowing through Him and the miracles He performed. I think they wanted what He had, so they asked him to teach them how to pray—to spell it out. Amazingly, prayer is the one thing Jesus actually taught his disciples how-to. It's almost like He knew we'd all have trouble communicating with a God we couldn't see and that most of our prayers would tend to be focused on our own needs and desires. So Jesus started with two prerequisites for prayer.

Your heart must be right. You shouldn't pray so others will see you and think you're super spiritual. Praying publicly is good, but only if you regularly pray in private.

You must be sincere. Babbling on to make sure you're heard or repeating the same prayer by rote is insincere and ineffective. God wants to hear what's on your heart.

In this passage from Matthew, commonly referred to as The Lord's Prayer, Jesus gives us Eight Principles of Prayer that will make our time with God transformational and meaningful.

1. *Position* (Matthew 6:9): First, God is our Father and we're part of His family. He's not some distant God who's bothered by us; instead, He loves to talk with us. Every detail of our life matters to Him, but the broader needs of His family (and ours) must also be our concern as we pray.
2. *Praise* (verse 9): He is the Creator of the universe—everything seen, unseen, and yet to be seen—and is worthy to be praised. His name is holy, and we lift His name up in adoration and awe. We give thanks for who He is and all that He's done. And we express our confidence in His great power.
3. *Purpose* (verse 10): Everybody wants their life to make a difference, and God wants us to invest in things that really matter. As we listen to God's nudging, we discover ways to serve others and share the love of Jesus.
4. *Petition* (verse 11): Even though He already knows what we need, God still wants us to ask. Asking creates dependence and a trust that He knows what's best for us. What Dad doesn't like to have his kids ask for help?

5. *Provision* (verse 11): God wants us to ask for daily bread—not just food but also a desire for His word. The truth of the Bible can change us, sustain us, and help us help others today.
6. *Pardon* (verse 12): Forgiveness is a wonderful gift, but God knows we're likely to hide when we sin. He wants us to be free from that guilt and weight, so regular and humble confession is important. So is eagerly extending forgiveness to those who wrong us.
7. *Path* (verse 13): Asking God to lead us implies we are ready to follow in His steps and His ways. This narrow road leads to life; there is no better path to take.
8. *Protection* (verse 13): The enemy is on the prowl and wants to tempt us and defeat us. He wants to destroy our character, divide our relationships, and discourage and derail us from experiencing God's best. Praying for protection for ourselves and others is an essential part of our daily walk.

Think of prayer as your lifeline to God. Using the "Eight Ps" will transform you—and your prayer life.

Be a WisdomWalker!

On average, how many minutes a day do you spend in prayer? What kind of praying do you do (is it before meals, in times of crisis, etc.)?

Why do you think Jesus told the disciples to pray a certain way? Which of the "Eight Ps" are you used to praying? Which ones are new to you?

Begin a prayer log of specific people, plans, and situations. Note the date you begin praying and the way God responds. What an awesome record of His faithfulness!

A Step Deeper

Live Intentionally. Maximize Your Relationships. Pass the Torch.

Live It

1. Spend some time with God in prayer.

2. Ask God to help you focus, free of distractions, as you pray the "Eight Ps."
3. Write down everything He tells you in the "My Insights" section.
4. Confess any wrongdoing and sinful behavior and ask Him to forgive you.
5. Ask Him to give you the courage and determination to change what needs to be changed.

Maximize It

1. Brainstorm ways to find more time for prayer.
2. Pray, following the "Eight Ps."
3. Discuss what you've learned about the way Jesus told His disciples to pray.

Pass It On

For additional study, read and reflect on:

- Luke 5:16; 11:1–13
- Ephesians 3:14–21

Share one of the above Scriptures with a friend or family member—and talk about how its wisdom and truth has influenced you to make some changes in your life.

My Insights

_____

_____

_____

_____

_____

_____

Father, thank You for giving me an example of prayer directly from Jesus. Thank You for giving me the freedom to express my heart and the focus to keep me from wandering. It's my desire to come to You every day and to let You change my heart and direct my steps.

32

CALLED TO GREATNESS

WisdomWalks Principle
God uses the few who are faith-full.

*It is the nature of man to rise to greatness
if greatness is expected of him.*

JOHN STEINBECK

I just love the US Marines. They defend freedom around the world. They train and sacrifice and endure the most brutal conditions imaginable, just so they're fully prepared for the enemy. They're first to fight and can respond in the trenches of the battlefield, in the depths of the water, and from the height of flight.

Through training, they *become* the best of the best. And they don't even pretend to be for everybody, but they are for the "few"—those willing to be transformed into the greatest fighting force in the world. Everything about the Marines breathes honor, courage, and commitment. They face fear and overcome it. And by the time their TV commercials are done, I'm ready to enlist; my soul has been stirred to pursue greatness.

Trying to compare the Old Testament Gideon's army with the Marines would be like comparing an orange to a horse. There would be almost no similarity...except for the fact that both were looking for a few good men.

WisdomWalking

When the angel of the LORD appeared to Gideon, he said, "The LORD is with you, mighty warrior.... Go in the strength you have and save Israel out of Midian's hand. Am I not sending you?" "But Lord," Gideon asked, "how can I save Israel? My clan is the weakest in Manasseh, and I am the least in my family." The LORD answered, "I will be with you, and you will strike down all the Midianites together."

JUDGES 6:12, 14–16

Gideon's army was definitely not a well-trained fighting machine. Gideon himself questioned God's choice because he was the least in his family and his clan was the weakest. He believed God could *do* nothing because he and his family *were* nothing! In Judges 7:2–7, when Gideon told his brave group that if they were afraid, then they could go home, 22,000 left! (Something tells me they were hustling to get out of there; they didn't want any possibility that Gideon was just kidding.) Their fear overcame any small amount of faith they may have possessed.

Then God made Gideon whittle the remaining 10,000 soldiers down to an intimidating fighting force of only *300 men*. Talk about "a few good men"! Are you kidding? To face the Midianites, who numbered over 100,000? And the 300 weren't even fierce warriors—they got chosen because they lapped water like dogs. God did not want them to boast in their own strength, so He created a situation where victory would only be possible through faith in God alone. And their faith overcame their fear!

Gideon and his men weren't chosen because they were capable. The task at hand was far beyond them. I believe He chose them to give us a real-life picture that proves "for when I am weak, then am I strong" (2 Corinthians 12:10). Whenever God calls us to a task that we think is beyond us, we must focus on the unlimited power of God, rather than our own limited resources and talent, for nothing is impossible with God (Luke 1:37). It's another reminder that life is a walk of faith.

God doesn't choose the few who are qualified; He qualifies the few that He chooses. When you are part of "the few":

You will grow to be completely dependent on Him. We often think God only uses the best of the best. But He does exactly the opposite. He chooses the "few" who have a humble, trusting heart. He chooses those who are willing to let His power flow through them.

Your faith will overcome your fear. You will have faith in God's power and promise instead of being fearful because of your weakness and worry. Gideon and the 300 men had faith that God would defeat the Midianites as promised, and He did.

As the Marines' motto says, *Semper Fidelis*, "always faithful," God is always faithful. Are you?

Be a WisdomWalker!

What is the one thing you would do if you were certain you would not fail? What is keeping you from doing that thing? Explain.

If you believed, "With God, everything is possible," how would that change your perspective on the one thing you'd like to do?

A Step Deeper

Live Intentionally. Maximize Your Relationships. Pass the Torch.

Live It

1. Spend some time with God in prayer.
2. Ask God to give you the desire to become one of the faithful "few."
3. Write down everything He tells you in the "My Insights" section.
4. Confess any wrongdoing and sinful behavior and ask Him to forgive you.
5. Ask Him to give you the courage and determination to change what needs to be changed.

Maximize It

1. Talk with a trusted friend or mentor about the everyday challenges you face that seem insurmountable right now.
2. Are you full of fear or faith? Are you more focused on your weakness or God's power? Explain. If you choose to be faithful, what might you accomplish?
3. Brainstorm some ways to tackle the one thing you decided you'd like to do in the "Be a WisdomWalker!" section.

Pass It On

For additional study, read and reflect on:

- Joshua 1:9
- John 16:33
- Romans 12:21
- 1 Corinthians 1:25–27

Share one of the above Scriptures with a friend or family member—and talk about how its wisdom and truth has influenced you to make some changes in your life.

My Insights

_____

_____

_____

_____

_____

_____

_____

_____

_____

Father, I know You have chosen me to be part of Your family by grace through faith in Your Son, Jesus. You have not chosen me because of my talent or goodness or worthiness. There was nothing I could do to qualify other than to put my faith in Christ. Help me to be "one of the few"—one of those faithful servants who depend on You fully and trust You to work in a mighty way. May Your strength be made perfect in my weakness as my faith overcomes my fear.

33

ONE WAY

WisdomWalks Principle
The path you pick leads to life or death.

*Efforts and courage are not enough
without purpose and direction.*

JOHN F. KENNEDY

One of my favorite movie scenes of all time is from the movie *Planes, Trains, and Automobiles.* John Candy and Steve Martin, complete strangers, meet in an airport when their flights get canceled because of a snowstorm. The movie is a hilarious story of their trek together as they try desperately to get home for the holidays.

There's one scene where John Candy tries to take off his winter coat while driving and ends up spinning the car round and round before coming to a stop. Steve Martin sleeps through the whole thing. When they get back on the highway, they are going the wrong way. Another driver desperately yells at them, "You're going the wrong way!" over and over again. But Martin and Candy laugh, make fun of him, and ask each other, "How do they know where we're going?" Before long, though, they see two eighteen-wheelers coming straight at them from the other direction. Their rental car is squeezed between the two trucks and completely destroyed. Martin and Candy narrowly escape with their lives. The car ends up bursting into flames as they watch from the side of the road.

It turns out they were indeed "going the wrong way." But they had no idea.

WisdomWalking

"Do not let your hearts be troubled. Trust in God; trust also in me. In my Father's house are many rooms; if it were not so, I would have told

you. I am going to prepare a place for you. And if I go and prepare a place for you, I will come back and take you to be with me that you also may be where I am. You know the way to the place where I am going." Thomas said to him, "Lord, we don't know where you are going, so how can we know the way?" Jesus answered, "I am the way and the truth and the life. No one comes to the Father except through me."

JOHN 14:1–6

Thomas and the rest of the disciples were concerned. Jesus was teaching hard things: He told them He was going to die. He predicted He would be betrayed by one of them. Then He said that Peter (part of his inner circle) would deny any association with Him. They were stunned and confused; they must have thought the whole Jesus movement was unraveling. So when Jesus started talking about leaving them and going away to His Father's house to prepare a place for them, they felt even more lost. How would they know where to find Him? How would they know which way to go?

We all want to know which way to go in life, don't we? At least nobody I know actually wants to go the wrong way. Funny thing, though—we're all convinced we're going the right way. Yet Proverbs 14:12 says that, in the end, what we think is the right way leads to death. There are many philosophies and religions that tell you all the things you need to do to go to heaven. In this age of tolerance and relative truth, you may hear a common phrase that "All roads lead to heaven." You may also hear "whatever works for you." But that isn't what Jesus teaches.

Jesus says that only one road leads to eternal life, to the Father's house. Jesus is the way, the truth, and the life, and no one comes to the Father except through Him. He didn't say "a" way; He said "the" way. He was reminding us to follow Him. It was the exact thing He'd said when He first called them: *"Follow me."* Wherever I go, follow in my footsteps. Do the things you see me do. Be the kind of person you see me being.

In John 3:36 we're told that whoever believes in the Son has eternal life, but whoever rejects the Son will not see life. And in 1 Timothy 2:5–6 we're told that Jesus is the one and only "mediator" between God and man. Jesus stands in the gap, arms stretched wide across the cross, so that everyone who believes in Him can have their relationship with God restored. He alone can make that connection possible. Not Mohammed. Not Buddha.

Not Joseph Smith. Not the gods of Hinduism. Not even our own efforts and good deeds.

So what do you believe? Is Jesus really "the" way? You decide. Pick a path. If you choose Jesus, you're compelled to follow Him, and that implies taking action…putting aside your desires in order to walk His way. But His way *always* leads to life—eternal life.

Be a WisdomWalker!

If you were to follow someone or imitate their life, how would you do it? How would you know how to talk, think, and act?

What's the difference between being a believer and being a follower? Are you a believer, a follower, or both? Why?

If all roads lead to heaven, what does that say about the ultimate sacrifice that Jesus made? What was it worth? Explain your answer.

A Step Deeper

Live Intentionally. Maximize Your Relationships. Pass the Torch.

Live It

1. Spend some time with God in prayer.
2. Ask God to help you understand fully Jesus' role as "mediator" between God and man.
3. Write down everything He tells you in the "My Insights" section.
4. Confess any wrongdoing and sinful behavior and ask Him to forgive you.
5. Ask Him to give you the courage and determination to change what needs to be changed.

Maximize It

1. Are you taking your own path or following in Jesus' footsteps with: the way you speak? your thoughts and attitudes? the way you treat others?
2. What does being a believer and a follower really mean to you? And what kind of spiritual transformation has it prompted in your life?
3. Do you believe there is only one way to heaven? And that your way is right? How can you be sure?

Pass It On

For additional study, read and reflect on:

- Proverbs 14:12
- Matthew 7:13–14
- John 8:57–59; 14:6
- Acts 4:1–12
- Philippians 2:9–11

Share one of the above Scriptures with a friend or family member—and talk about how its wisdom and truth has influenced you to make some changes in your life.

My Insights

_____

_____

_____

_____

_____

Father, I believe that Jesus is the way, the truth, and the life, and that no one comes to You any other way. That every other way is the wrong way and leads to death. I understand that through Your Son's death on the cross, He paid the price for my sins and bridged the gap to eternal life. I know that Your way leads to life. Help me to follow where You lead me. I desire to walk in Your way. Amen.

34

FAILURE IS NOTHING

WisdomWalks Principle
Admit it, forget it, and get back in it.

I've missed more than 9,000 shots in my career. I've lost almost 300 games.
Twenty-six times I've been trusted to take the game winning shot and missed.
I've failed over and over in my life. And that is why I succeed.

MICHAEL JORDAN

In my early teens, I had an opportunity to play on an All-Star baseball team that won all the way to the championship game. When I came up to bat with the winning run on second base, I had a perfect opportunity to win the game.

I ripped the first pitch from the big lefty down the left field line scoring two runs for the win—or so I thought. The umpire signaled a very late foul ball call, and the runners returned. The next two pitches were inside-out fastballs that froze my bat to my shoulder and ended our chance for the win. I had failed the team.

At that moment, I had a choice. I could let that failure end my love and pursuit of baseball—or I could use it to drive me to get better. Although I was discouraged, I chose to let that failure fuel my future success.

People have failed all throughout history. I did. Peter, one of Jesus' closest friends, did. And you will, too. But it's what we *do after that failure* that defines us and our future.

WisdomWalking

Peter replied [to Jesus], "Even if all fall away on account of you, I never will." "I tell you the truth," Jesus answered, "this very night, before the rooster crows, you will disown me three times." But Peter declared,

> *"Even if I have to die with you, I will never disown you." And all the other disciples said the same.... [Later, after Peter denied knowing Jesus three times] immediately a rooster crowed. Then Peter remembered the word Jesus had spoken: "Before the rooster crows, you will disown me three times." And he went outside and wept bitterly.*

MATTHEW 26:33–35, 74–75

Peter, along with James and John, formed Jesus' inner circle and saw things no one else got to see. They were special. Yet when that rooster crowed, Peter was crushed by a failure he said would never happen. Oh, how the mighty fall! This couldn't be Peter, the confident one.

Yet, it was Peter. The enemy was hard at work, trying to take down one of the mighty men of Jesus. His plan was to *discourage, defeat,* and *define* Peter's very identity by his failure. Satan knew that, if he was successful, Peter would be reminded of his past failures and be unlikely to attempt great things in the future.

Many people today point to Peter as an example of all the things you don't want to do: speaking before you think, having little faith, being impulsive, and shrinking back and denying he ever knew Jesus. They see him as a failure. But that's not what Jesus saw. He could see the future through Peter's failures. He knew what kind of spiritual warrior Peter would become, and that he would use Peter as the very foundation of a movement that would change the course of history.

Peter failed. I will fail. You will fail. But there are three things we can do so that today's failures don't disrupt the future God has planned for us:

Admit it. When you fail, come clean. Hiding sin doesn't work; God already knows what you did or said or failed to do. "Admit it" means see it for what it is, repent from it and resolve to turn away, ask God to forgive you, learn from it, and make it right with whomever you need to. When Peter blew it, he knew instantly. He didn't hesitate to admit it and make it right.

Forget it. Once you've admitted it, let it go. When you hear reminders in your head, stop them in their tracks. God doesn't keep a list of things you've already been forgiven of, and neither should you. After Jesus forgave Peter and restored him, Peter was free from the weight of guilt and able to forget it and move on.

Get back in it. Once you're forgiven, it's over. In Philippians 3:13–14, Paul said to press on toward the goal. Peter overcame his shame and literally ran to see the empty tomb. Shortly after that, he was preaching to the masses and thousands believed. Don't waste any time. Get back in the game!

God wants you to live fully, without being weighed down by shame and guilt. Proverbs 24:16 says, "Even though the righteous man falls seven times, he will rise again." Don't let failure keep you down. Admit it. Forget it. And get back in it! Use the failure to fuel your future successes. God has too much to accomplish through you for you to be burdened by past failures.

Be a WisdomWalker!

What areas of sin or failure are you holding on to? *Admit it.* Take just five minutes (or however long it takes) to write those things down. Confess your sin.

What is God telling you to do about each sin or failure? What do you need to do to make them right?

What two or three moments from the past keep coming back to mind, over and over again? How can you *forget it?*

A Step Deeper

Live Intentionally. Maximize Your Relationships. Pass the Torch.

Live It

1. Spend some time with God in prayer.
2. Ask God to reveal areas of sin and failure you're holding on to.
3. Write down everything He tells you in the "My Insights" section.
4. Confess any wrongdoing and sinful behavior and ask Him to forgive you.
5. Ask Him to give you the courage and determination to change what needs to be changed.

Maximize It

1. Ask a trusted friend to step in and remind you that you're forgiven and free from the weight of the past when it circles around again.
2. Discuss with that friend what might be next. What do you believe God is asking you to do now that you've been hesitant to do?
3. Brainstorm ways you can get the above task done, and make a commitment with your friend to do it.

Pass It On

For additional study, read and reflect on:

- Proverbs 24:16
- John 20:1–9; 21:15–19
- Philippians 3:7–14
- 1 John 1:5–10

Share one of the above Scriptures with a friend or family member—and talk about how its wisdom and truth has influenced you to make some changes in your life.

My Insights

_____

_____

_____

_____

_____

Father, I know I have failed many times, but You don't want me to be weighed down by the past. Reveal to me sin that I have not confessed so I can admit it, forget it, and get back in it. Help me to make it right with those I have wronged. I know no failure is beyond Your forgiveness, and I'm thankful You are faithful to forgive and restore. Help me to be willing to attempt great things for You, Lord, with no fear of failure. I will follow as You lead.

35

PUMP IT UP!

WisdomWalks Principle
Stay connected to the Source.

Christ is the key to every spiritual blessing.
He alone fulfills the deepest longings of our hearts
and supplies every spiritual resource we need.

JOHN MACARTHUR

A few months ago, as I started my morning routine, I quickly discovered there was no water coming from the faucet. My suspicion that our ten-year-old-well pump had finally given up was confirmed by the plumber, who informed me it would cost $2,500 to replace it and restore water flow to our house.

While I haven't had a lot of success with past plumbing projects, I decided to "do it myself" (I'm just that kind of guy) and save about $2,000. For plumbing, electrical, and car issues, the term *do-it-myself* means, "Call my brother!"

It took us a full three days to pull the pump 240 feet up and out of the well and replace the pump. Other friends from the neighborhood came as we worked late into the evenings; it looked like a full-blown rescue operation! We decided to test it before we lowered it back into the ground and, you guessed it, it didn't work. Turns out the pump was fine, but the electrical connection was cut.

I found out in those few days just how dependent we are on running water. We couldn't use the toilets, shower, brush our teeth, wash dishes, or wash clothes. Life came to a grinding halt because we had no connection to the water source.

If you're not experiencing a growing portion of love, joy, peace, patience, kindness, goodness, faithfulness, gentleness, and self-control in your life, perhaps it's time to pump up your connection to the Source.

I am the true vine, and my Father is the gardener. He cuts off every branch in me that bears no fruit, while every branch that does bear fruit he prunes so that it will be even more fruitful. You are already clean because of the word I have spoken to you. Remain in me, and I will remain in you. No branch can bear fruit by itself; it must remain in the vine. Neither can you bear fruit unless you remain in me. I am the vine; you are the branches. If a man remains in me and I in him, he will bear much fruit; apart from me you can do nothing.

JOHN 15:1-5

Life also comes to a grinding halt when you lose your connection to Jesus. In fact, Jesus said that apart from Him, you can do nothing. In other words, your life will bear no fruit. Sure, it may seem to go on as usual. In fact, you may look pretty successful on the outside…great job, nice house, solid reputation, good kids. But that's not success as Jesus defines it. What does a life-giving connection to Jesus look like?

The vine is the source of life for the branches. If the branch gets cut off from the vine, it dies. It can't be disconnected at any time. Otherwise it can't get the nutrients it needs for life, and it will have no chance to bear fruit. Money, stuff, success, adventures, relationships, and pleasure won't fully satisfy us, because they're not designed to. Only a relationship with Jesus can provide meaning and purpose.

Staying connected to Jesus is our responsibility. When we stay connected to Jesus, He grows us and shows us His way. As we *seek Him*, as we *pray and meditate on His Word*, as we *offer Him praise and worship*, and as we *love and serve others*, our love for Christ grows.

A branch with big leaves may look impressive, but for that branch to stay alive and grow, it's all about the fruit. Bearing fruit is a collaborative effort. It's the Father's job to tend to the branches to produce the most fruit possible. It's our job to connect to Jesus and allow Him to care for and prune us so we can continue to grow.

As you allow God access to everything—your pain and disappointment, your hopes and dreams, your relationships, your attitudes and actions—He'll be faithful to lovingly prune you so you can bear life-giving fruit. After all, He *is* the expert.

Be a WisdomWalker!

How would you describe your connection with Jesus? Is it distant, inconsistent, intimate, something else? What makes it that way?

What do you learn during your "connection" times with Jesus? What does He reveal to you?

What specific things can you do to make the connection more clear and consistent? List them.

A Step Deeper

Live Intentionally. Maximize Your Relationships. Pass the Torch.

Live It

1. Spend some time with God in prayer.
2. Ask God to give you the desire to increase your connection time with Him.
3. Write down everything He tells you in the "My Insights" section.
4. Confess any wrongdoing and sinful behavior and ask Him to forgive you.
5. Ask Him to give you the courage and determination to change what needs to be changed.

Maximize It

1. With a friend brainstorm ideas for increasing your connection time with God. What might you have to reorganize in order to make that happen?

2. Write a commitment to God:

   On this day, I commit to stay connected with You by....

   Sign and date it. Have your friend or mentor cosign it as a witness, and date it. Keep this commitment where you will see it each morning.

Pass It On
For additional study, read and reflect on:

- Romans 1:11–16
- 2 Corinthians 6:3–10; 9:6–13
- Galatians 5:22–23; 6:2
- Colossians 1:10
- Hebrews 13:15

Share one of the above Scriptures with a friend or family member—and talk about how its wisdom and truth has influenced you to make some changes in your life.

My Insights

_____

_____

_____

_____

_____

_____

Father, I know that in order for my life to bear fruit, I must remain connected to You through an intimate relationship with Jesus. It's my desire to do whatever it takes to seek You and spend time with You. I know that as I spend time getting to know You through prayer, worship, and the Word, You will meet me where I am, and You will begin to prune me and transform my heart and my life into what it's intended to be. As I connect, I pray that I will bear much fruit.

36

A 4-FOOT-9 GIANT

WisdomWalks Principle
Do everything you can to change someone's world.

*Do all the good you can, by all the means you can,
in all the ways you can, in all the places you can,
at all the times you can, to all the people you can, as long as ever you can.*

JOHN WESLEY

When you think of undying, unwavering commitment, what person comes first to your mind? For me, that person is a four-foot, nine-inch, sixty-one-year-old grandma. I know what you're thinking: *That's not the image of commitment that came to my mind.* It wasn't mine, either, until I met her in South Korea this past summer at FCA's first-ever South Korea Sports Camp. Su-Ja Parks (I called her Grandma Parks) is a youth pastor in Seoul, and she's been working with and encouraging young people for thirty-seven years.

Grandma Parks caught my eye the first day by the way she was "jumping" into the icebreakers and sports competition. Her enthusiasm was contagious. All day long, she loved on the girls in her Huddle group. At the soccer clinic, she played and participated in every drill. She had never played soccer before, but she announced with a beaming smile, "I am younger today for playing." Each night, I watched her worship God with incredible passion. She prayed over the kids nonstop, interceding with God on their behalf. One night she was on her knees on the wood floor for over an hour. She had to be helped up by two people, and it took her several minutes before she could stand on her own.

Meeting Grandma Parks marked my life. What gripped me so intensely was her commitment to the kids and to the Lord. Year after year, she served the youth in her church. At first I'd thought she was just an old lady who volunteered for the camp. Little did I know that this petite grandma was a spiritual giant, called by God to bring life change—in those kids' lives, and in my own.

May the Master pour on the love so it fills your lives and splashes over on everyone around you, just as it does from us to you. May you be infused with strength and purity, filled with confidence in the presence of God our Father when our Master Jesus arrives with all his followers.

1 THESSALONIANS 3:12–13 MSG

If anyone could embody 1 Thessalonians 3:12–13, it would be Grandma Parks.

I was:

- Amazed by her faithfulness.
- Humbled by her impact.
- Humiliated for judging her as just a grandma (and rightfully so!).
- Honored to meet her.
- Blessed when she prayed over me.
- Changed because I met her.
- Motivated by her service.
- Challenged by her commitment.
- Convicted by her passion.

My greatest desire is to be found faithful, like Grandma Parks. I am convinced that the Lord says to her at the end of every day, "Well done, good and faithful servant!" She is my new hero. I am grateful beyond measure that the Lord brought her into my life, for she indeed has taught me what undying, unwavering commitment is all about.

Be a WisdomWalker!

Do you know someone who reminds you of Grandma Parks? Someone who has been faithful over the years? If so, what characteristics about this person amaze you? What draws you to them?

What makes this person so unusual? What is it in their life story or their spiritual disciplines that have so shaped them?

How would you describe your own spiritual commitment?

A Step Deeper

Live Intentionally. Maximize Your Relationships. Pass the Torch.

Live It

1. Spend some time with God in prayer.
2. Ask God to reveal areas where you're waffling and to give you the desire for unwavering, undying commitment.
3. Write down everything He tells you in the "My Insights" section.
4. Confess any wrongdoing and sinful behavior and ask Him to forgive you.
5. Ask Him to give you the courage and determination to change what needs to be changed.

Maximize It

1. What eternal impact would you like to make? Tell those hopes to a trusted friend or mentor.
2. Ask that friend how he or she would describe your spiritual commitment.
3. How closely does that perspective match how you described your own spiritual commitment in "Be a WisdomWalker!"? If there are discrepancies, why do you think that's the case?

4. In 1 Thessalonians 3:12, Paul shared how our love needs to overflow. What are several ways God can use you to splash Christ's love onto others?

Pass It On
For additional study, read and reflect on:

• 1 Timothy 1:5; 6:11

Share one of the above Scriptures with a friend or family member—and talk about how its wisdom and truth has influenced you to make some changes in your life.

My Insights

_____

_____

_____

_____

_____

_____

_____

_____

_____

Lord Jesus, I want to be found faithful like Grandma Parks. Teach me what it means to have undying, unwavering commitment for You alone, Lord. So many times I waver in my faith. I have so many fears and doubts. During these times of second-guessing, strengthen my faith and encourage my heart. May my love for You overflow into others' lives. In Jesus' name I pray. Amen.

37

IT'S CONTAGIOUS!

WisdomWalks Principle
Make your life worth catching.

con·ta·gious (kən'tājəs) adjective
  ¹ Capable of being transmitted or spread from one
    person to another by direct or indirect contact.
    Easily spread, passed on, or caught.
  ² Synonym—Infectious.

My wife can be a little obsessed with germs. (I think that's safe to say, because she'd agree wholeheartedly with me.) She makes everyone in the family use antibacterial soaps. She packs a hand-sanitizer in the kids' lunch boxes for school. And when we travel by plane, she wipes down the seat, armrests, seat belt, call buttons, and even the tray table. I must admit, even though I'm embarrassed by her actions sometimes, I very rarely get sick when I travel now.

It's amazing to me just how far we've come since the days when moms would make sure that if one of the kids got the chickenpox, then the rest would get put in the same room to get it at the same time. If one of our kids got it now, my wife would set up a quarantine room and vacuum-seal the door. You can just imagine what my wife did when news of the H1N1 virus hit, and we were warned of a worldwide pandemic…. And she wasn't the only one; the whole world got crazy in an effort to prevent the Swine Flu.

But everything about us is contagious, and that's true in the spiritual life, as well. God made us to be contagious! How you live *will be* caught by others—for better or for worse. Others will catch your emotions, your attitudes, and even your way of thinking, because it usually surfaces in your words and your entire approach to life.

The apostle Paul had a lot to say about contagious faith.

We always thank God, the Father of our Lord Jesus Christ, when we pray for you, because we have heard of your faith in Christ Jesus and the love you have for all the saints—the faith and love that spring from the hope that is stored up for you in heaven and that you have already heard about in the Word of truth, the gospel that has come to you. All over the world this faith is bearing fruit and growing.

COLOSSIANS 1:3–6

Good news spreads! The faith and love of the saints in Colosse, like that of those in Rome (Romans 1:8) was highly contagious. It was literally being reported around the world. Faith in Jesus and the Gospel of salvation by grace was bearing fruit and spreading. When people hear about the presence of God in your life and see the difference with their own eyes, that's a powerfully attractive combination! What you believe can be caught. Faith and belief in God, when consistently lived out in your actions and words, can be passed on from friend to friend, family to family, and generation to generation.

Bad news paralyzes! Bad news spreads like a plague. It always brings others down and starts a cycle of negativity. In Numbers 13, fear swept through the entire nation of Israel as they prepared to enter the Promised Land. Two young scouts, Joshua and Caleb, gave a good report, but the other ten spread doubt and fear all through the camp. As a result, the entire community grumbled against Moses and Aaron and even suggested that they should go back to slavery in Egypt—all because a little bad news paralyzed them!

Bad behavior breeds! In 1 Corinthians 5 the church was a mess. They were engaging in immoral behavior and even bragging about it. So what did Paul do? He told them to cut it out! He said their sinful behavior was spreading like a little yeast through a batch of dough. He told believers to have nothing to do with believers engaged in these behaviors because they themselves might be corrupted.

Thankfully, God gave us a physical, mental, emotional, and spiritual immune system. And the healthier we keep that immune system, the more capable we are to fight off the bad "viruses" we encounter. What are you doing to boost your own personal immune system spiritually so you don't "catch" all the sick stuff you may encounter?

Your life *is* contagious—one way or the other. What will you pass on to others?

Be a WisdomWalker!

Draw a line down the center of a piece of paper. At the top, label the left side of the page "Healthy" and the right side "Sick." Consider your attitude, words, actions, thoughts, and emotions, and the people you come in contact with regularly.

What specific things are you passing on to others that are healthy? (List on the left side.)

What specific things are you passing on to others that are sick? (List on the right side.)

A Step Deeper

Live Intentionally. Maximize Your Relationships. Pass the Torch.

Live It

1. Spend some time with God in prayer.
2. Ask God to reveal to you where your spiritual immune system needs a boost.
3. Write down everything He tells you in the "My Insights" section.
4. Confess any wrongdoing and sinful behavior and ask Him to forgive you.
5. Ask Him to give you the courage and determination to change what needs to be changed.

Maximize It

1. Look at your "Healthy" and "Sick" lists with a trusted friend or mentor. On each side, circle one thing that, if you were more intentional about it, would have the most dramatic positive impact on you and others.
2. Why would each of these two things make such a large change in your own and others' lives?
3. What can you do to boost your spiritual immune system so you stop the virus before the infection sets in?

Pass It On

For additional study, read and reflect on:

- Acts 4:20
- Romans 1:8
- 1 Corinthians 5:6–8
- Galatians 5:7–9
- Colossians 1

Share one of the above Scriptures with a friend or family member—and talk about how its wisdom and truth has influenced you to make some changes in your life.

My Insights

_____

_____

_____

_____

Father, relationships are at the core of who You are. I know You designed me to be contagious and that just about everything in my life can be caught by others. I want to be positively contagious, so others catch my faith in Jesus and His unconditional love, so they catch joy and enthusiasm, peace and kindness, generosity and courage. Please continue to change me on the inside, so I can encourage others to be healthy, too.

38

GOING, GOING...GONE

WisdomWalks Principle
Live light and free on earth.
Hold tight to heaven.

My home is in heaven.
I'm just traveling through this world.
BILLY GRAHAM

On November 20, 2006, five-time Olympic champion Ian Thorpe retired from competitive swimming at the age of twenty-four. He said that breaking records "wasn't as inspiring as it should have been." As a teenager, Thorpe splashed into the swimming scene and made thirteen world records between 1999 and 2002, then became an international star after dominating at the Sydney Olympics.

It didn't take long for Thorpe to realize that success wasn't all it's cracked up to be. Medals, titles, records, and accomplishments didn't last long. The fans went home. The cameras were turned off. And Thorpe was left with an empty feeling—even after breaking all those world records. Proof indeed that what's seen is temporary. It never lasts, and it's never enough to satisfy.

We spend so much time on the here and now. Yet compared to eternity, life on earth is like a couple of seconds. In James 4:13–14, we are warned about the brevity of life, "Come now, you who say, 'Today or tomorrow we will travel to such and such a city and spend a year there and do business and make a profit.' You don't even know what tomorrow will bring—what your life will be! For you are a bit of smoke that appears for a little while, then vanishes" (HCSB).

Could you imagine staying in a hotel for a night and replacing the room's contents with your own furniture and pictures? Setting it up like it was your home? Maybe even getting a nice, big-screen TV for better viewing? People would consider you nuts to go to that extreme for one night, wouldn't they? I'm sure God looks at us in the same way: "Hey, why are you are so consumed with your few seconds on earth? You are spending incredible amount of time and money on the very things that won't last."

WisdomWalking

So we do not focus on what is seen, but on what is unseen; for what is seen is temporary, but what is unseen is eternal.

2 CORINTHIANS 4:18 HCSB

Why does Paul encourage us to focus on the unseen, even if it sounds a little crazy? Because what's in the seen (the world) won't last. As a twenty-four-year-old, Ian Thorpe realized something: *Blink, and all those achievements are gone.* If your focus is on the seen, you'll hold onto things too tightly and will live a hard life as a result. If your focus is on the unseen, you'll hold things lightly, and you will live free.

This life is a vapor…a mist. Going, going…gone. That's our life on earth.

This concept hit home for me when I noticed a book on heaven next to my father's bedside. One of his good friends had dropped it off to encourage him in his battle against leukemia. I asked him if he'd read it, and he smiled. "Why do I need to read about it when I will be experiencing it shortly?"

Perspective changes when you know you're coming closer to the end. And that was so true of my father. He realized his life was a bit of smoke that would vanish quickly, so he held this world loosely. In that, there was freedom and peace. Death didn't have a hold on his life, nor did this earth.

So why not swallow a healthy dose of heaven daily? Set your mind on things above. Don't get weighed down by what's temporary. Live free.

Be a WisdomWalker!

What have you won in the past that was significant at the time, but now is no big deal? What changed from then to now, and why?

Light a match, then blow it out. Count how many seconds the smoke lasts. That's the time James 4:14 mentions regarding the length of your life. How does this short exercise change the way you view your stay on earth?

What person in your life is a great example of someone who focuses on heaven? Why?

A Step Deeper

Live Intentionally. Maximize Your Relationships. Pass the Torch.

Live It

1. Spend some time with God in prayer.
2. Ask God to help you focus on what's unseen instead of what's seen.
3. Write down everything He tells you in the "My Insights" section.
4. Confess any wrongdoing and sinful behavior and ask Him to forgive you.
5. Ask Him to give you the courage and determination to change what needs to be changed.

Maximize It

1. Why is it so easy to focus on what's "seen" (the world we live in)?
2. Why is it so hard to focus on what's "unseen" (heaven)?

3. With a trusted mentor or friend brainstorm several ideas for keeping your focus on what's unseen.

Pass It On

For additional study, read and reflect on:

- Philippians 3:20–21
- James 4:13–14
- Revelation 4:2–8; 21:4

Share one of the above Scriptures with a friend or family member—and talk about how its wisdom and truth has influenced you to make some changes in your life.

My Insights

_____

_____

_____

_____

_____

_____

_____

_____

_____

Lord, I want to live for You alone. I am committed to focus on the unseen, not the seen. Help me to remove the things that blur my vision. To hold lightly to anything in the here and now. Too often I dwell on what's external instead of what really matters and on what's temporary instead of what's eternal. Show me that all I need is You. Confirm in my heart that this world is not my home, but that heaven—my true home—awaits.

39

WHAT'S FILLING YOU?

WisdomWalks Principle
Be controlled by the Spirit, not your-self.

*You can be full of the Spirit or full of your self,
but you can't be full of both.*

JIMMY PAGE

I love the little yellow warning light that alerts me when I'm almost out of gas. One of the cars we used to own even told us how many miles we had until empty. And trust me, I would push that right to the limit. But the car I drive now has the warning light, but no miles-to-empty warning. So I've made it into a game of sorts: just how far can I push it before I run out of gas?

Well so far, I've lost the game two or three times and had to call my wife to help me roadside. It really isn't any fun to run out of gas. The engine sputters briefly, then cuts off entirely. I'm left with virtually no brakes and a struggle with my "powerless" power-steering to get to the side of the road. Talk about living on the edge!

Everybody knows a car can't run without gas. It has no power. And even if everything else looks good, all the other fluids are topped off, the tires are filled with air, and the battery is fully charged, without gas the car simply won't go anywhere.

So much has been written about the purpose-driven life, but living on purpose—if it's missing one key ingredient—is like trying to drive your car on an empty gas tank! That one key ingredient, the gas that fuels the car, is the Holy Spirit. I've found the concept of being filled with the Holy Spirit, or walking with the very presence of God, to be hard to grasp. How about you?

The LORD replied, "My Presence will go with you, and I will give you rest." Then Moses said to him, "If your Presence does not go with us, do not send us up from here. How will anyone know that you are pleased with me and with your people unless you go with us? What else will distinguish me and all your people from all the other people on the face of the earth?"

EXODUS 33:14–16

Moses knew he needed God's presence—he'd experienced both life with it and life without it. He'd witnessed firsthand how God went ahead in the pillar of cloud by day and pillar of fire by night as they escaped from the Egyptians. He had witnessed the parting of the Red Sea by the presence and power of God. Moses knew that apart from God, the Israelites would be powerless again, so he wasn't taking any chances going forward.

But what does that mean for you? How do you fill your spiritual tank? How do you get the presence of God to go with you? Following Jesus' death and resurrection, the Spirit of God would no longer come and go as He did before. Instead, when we place our faith in Christ, the Holy Spirit now lives in us (John 14:15–26). But we can diminish His role by trying to do things in our own strength.

The word *filled* means two things:

Completed by. You hold nothing back. You give Him access to everything, and He gives you everything you need—for the decisions you'll make, the challenges you'll face, the relationships you have, etc. He will satisfy and complete you like nothing else can.

Controlled by. The Spirit directs your steps: He leads you, you listen to His voice, and obey (Galatians 5:16–18). You deliberately choose to lay down your life so He can live through you (Galatians 2:20). You receive His correction and conviction when you need it. While He never condemns, He does confront—yet only to bring transformational life-change. When you surrender control, you're saying, "Lord, take full control of my mind, my emotions, my words, and my actions." The life of a person who is completed by and controlled by the Holy Spirit enjoys the fruit of that filling—love, joy, peace, patience, kindness, goodness, faithfulness, gentleness, and self-control (Galatians 5:22–25), as well as wisdom, courage, and power (Acts 4–7).

Now *that's* the kind of life I want. What's filling you?

Be a WisdomWalker!

Squeeze a sponge tightly in your hand, then submerge it into water. Keep your fist tight at first (symbolizing our desire to be in control). Gradually release your grip and allow the water to fill every pore of the sponge (symbolizing your gradual surrender to God's control). The water symbolizes the filling of the Spirit. How would you describe your degree of surrender? Tight-fisted? Open-handed? Somewhere in-between? Why?

How much of your life have you opened up to God? In what areas?

What are you still holding on to?

A Step Deeper

Live Intentionally. Maximize Your Relationships. Pass the Torch.

Live It

1. Spend some time with God in prayer.
2. Ask God to help you empty yourself, so the Holy Spirit can fill your tank.
3. Write down everything He tells you in the "My Insights" section.
4. Confess any wrongdoing and sinful behavior and ask Him to forgive you.
5. Ask Him to give you the courage and determination to change what needs to be changed.

Maximize It

1. Discuss with a trusted friend or mentor what being "completed by" and "controlled by" the Holy Spirit means. How are you doing in each of these areas?
2. Look at the areas of life that you're still trying to control. Why is it so difficult for you to let go of those areas?
3. Pray together, asking God to help you let go, so you can be filled with and led by the Spirit.

Pass It On

For additional study, read and reflect on:

- 1 Samuel 10:6
- Isaiah 11:1–5
- Luke 4:1
- Acts 4:8–13
- Romans 8:1–17
- Galatians 5:22–25

Share one of the above Scriptures with a friend or family member—and talk about how its wisdom and truth has influenced you to make some changes in your life.

My Insights

_____

_____

_____

_____

Father, take full control of my mind, my emotions, my words, and my actions. I want my life-tank to be overflowing with You. Show me my sin so I can repent and surrender control of every area. Fill me with Your Spirit, so I can have the wisdom, courage, and power to live for You. May I reflect the fruits of Your Spirit to others.

THE GREATEST GIFT

WisdomWalks Principle
Live every day like it's your last.

*Few of us are called to do great things,
but many of us can do small things in a great way.*

UNKNOWN

My father, Edward T. Britton, who was also my best friend, passed away at 7:52 a.m. on May 2, 2008. Eight days later, on May 10, more than 1,100 people attended his Celebration Service to honor a life well lived. It was an incredible evening of laughing and crying, as we not only lifted up a man who impacted thousands during his lifetime but also celebrated the Lord Jesus Christ. Throughout my dad's journey with leukemia, he always talked about God's goodness, God's greatness, and God's graciousness. He was so thankful for his life and God's rich blessings.

Dad's faith was so solid that he didn't allow his circumstances to define him. In fact, his faith never wavered through the entire sickness, which lasted almost two years. He never once asked why God let this happen to him. He said he didn't have the right to ask. Instead he asked, "What?" What did the Lord want him to learn during this trial?

My dad stayed the course. He maintained the mission. He was totally focused on finishing well. Every time I called him during the last two months of life to ask how he was doing, he would say, "Contending." It was his way to say that he was fighting the good fight; running the right race. His focus can be best described by a journal entry he wrote on his CaringBridge site on January 25, 2008:

I continue serving and marching with the King daily. I'm absolutely convinced that I'm able to convey this positive update due to the serious and ongoing prayers of all of you! I am enjoying daily the final laps of my "retirement." May HE be ever present in your daily lives, starting with a serious quiet time in the mornings.

Right to the end, my father was focused on God's presence...and on getting to know Him more fully.

WisdomWalking

How can I repay the LORD for all his goodness to me?

PSALM 116:12

Psalm 116:12 was one of my father's favorite verses. He believed it, and lived out every second of the day as if it were his last. Not just when he became sick, but throughout his entire life. His favorite quote was, "Life is God's gift to us. What we do with it is our gift back to Him." He desired to repay the Lord with the way he lived his life. That became his life ambition.

What a great challenge for all of us who still have life! Are you taking life for granted? Not realizing how special it is until a loved one passes away?

The key is not only to understand this gift of life God has given us but also that how we live it is our gift back to Him. What are you doing with your life? Is it a blessing to God? Are you investing your life in things that please God? Are you ready to say, "Lord, I give to You my entire being—every action and decision, all my hopes and dreams, my thoughts and talk. I surrender it all back to You. May my life be a gift that brings You pleasure"?

Your life is indeed God's gift to you. But what you do with it is your gift back to Him! What would you like that gift to be?

Be a WisdomWalker!

If God is God, and He doesn't need anything, why do you think He needs you to give Him your life?

Do you see life as a gift from God? Why or why not?

If you could somehow package your life up as a gift and give it to God, what kind of gift would it be? Why?

A Step Deeper

Live Intentionally. Maximize Your Relationships. Pass the Torch.

Live It

1. Spend some time with God in prayer.
2. Ask God to help you begin to see your life as a gift *from* God—and also as a gift *to* God.
3. Write down everything He tells you in the "My Insights" section.
4. Confess any wrongdoing and sinful behavior and ask Him to forgive you.
5. Ask Him to give you the courage and determination to change what needs to be changed.

Maximize It

1. Read Psalm 116:12 with a trusted friend. How could this verse impact your life on a daily basis if you lived out its truth? Be specific.
2. Why do you think it's sometimes hard to see life as a gift from God? What gets in the way?
3. Discuss together how your life can be a gift *from* God and also *to God.* How does this perspective transform your thoughts, words, and actions?

Pass It On

For additional study, read and reflect on:

- Ephesians 5:15–21
- Colossians 4:5
- 2 Peter 1:3–11

Share one of the above Scriptures with a friend or family member—and talk about how its wisdom and truth has influenced you to make some changes in your life.

My Insights

_____

_____

_____

_____

_____

_____

_____

_____

_____

Jesus, I want my life to bring You pleasure. You know the deep yearnings in my heart to please You. So often my sin prevents me from loving You and others the way I should. At times I feel like my life is not a good gift for You. Please forgive me for the times that my life does not bring You honor and glory. I give You my life, as a gift, as is. Help me to live for You. Thank You, Lord. I love You. Amen.

YOU CAN DO IT!

In fact, you're already doing it.

Change is inevitable.
Transformation is a lifelong pursuit.

DAN BRITTON AND JIMMY PAGE

Since you started reading *WisdomWalks*, you may have discovered something profound: that the most memorable moments happen in the midst of real life. Wisdom isn't something you wait to acquire when you get "old." Wisdom is passed on in everyday moments, through everyday events, and by everyday people, like you and me, who are willing to be intentional. Everything you experience is an opportunity to dig deeper, to connect the dots of faith and life, and to pass on your most important beliefs.

That's exactly how Jesus turned the world upside down and started a worldwide movement of people who put their faith in action. These people saw their relationship with Jesus as an intricate part of their lives. They didn't join God's team to sit on the bench. They had a desire to make a contribution. Their thoughts, their words, the way they did business, interacted with their neighbors, handled temptation, you name it, all reflected their faith and the condition of their hearts.

Jesus didn't just let life happen. He was intentional. Whether He was walking on the paths, telling stories, teaching to a crowd, eating a meal in the upper room, or healing the sick, Jesus was walking wisdom: The Wisdom That Walks! He taught His followers to be intentional too. Through His parables, He passed on the wisdom of God. You can too. In fact, it's *crucial* you do. More people than you know are counting on you.

Jesus IS Wisdom—Get Jesus!

For our benefit God made [Christ] to be wisdom itself.
Christ made us right with God; he made us pure and
holy, and he freed us from sin.

1 CORINTHIANS 1:30 NLT

The *WisdomWalks* experience is a perfect blend of mentoring, discipleship, and accountability—all significant benefits of a growing relationship. All you need is a desire to walk with Jesus personally and to bring another person with you.

In a *mentoring* relationship, the mentor is the teacher, who has more life experience and desires to pass on in-the-trenches wisdom to the next generation. The one being mentored has the opportunity to capitalize on what the mentor has learned, avoid similar mistakes, and implement principles and practices with a proven track record.

In a *discipleship* relationship, the mentor is a sage—someone who has spiritual maturity. The focus is on spiritual training and growth, using the study and application of God's Word in every circumstance and life area. More than a teacher-student relationship, it follows the model of what Jesus did: He lived out the truth and taught it at the same time.

In an *accountability* relationship, the mentor is a friend. There is a mutual mentoring with each person completely committed to helping the other become everything God intends. Both are committed to help the other stay true to what God has called them to do. Attitudes and actions are confronted firmly and lovingly. Every area of life is open for discussion. There's a transparency that allows real transformation to happen.

WisdomWalker

Main Entry: wis·dom·walker
Pronunciation: ˈwizdəmˈwôker
Function: noun
Date: 2010
[1] one who creates intentional, spiritual, life-changing connections.

*Mentoring means personal,
passionate commitment to Jesus.*

DAN BRITTON

WisdomWalks is more than just teachable moments—it's an experience so profound it will transform your life and the lives of those around you. If you've navigated your way through *WisdomWalks* with another, take a look back at all the things you've learned and the wisdom you've gained. Because of your relational intentionality, you've lived life deeper, haven't you? Look at the memories you've made. And surprise! By just walking alongside others through *WisdomWalks*, you're already involved in the mentoring process!

If instead you use *WisdomWalks* for your own personal growth, why not go for it and become a WisdomWalker? Show others through your life, your relationships, and your faith what it looks like to walk with Jesus. Decide, *No more sitting on the sidelines and letting life happen. I'm going to be a catalyst for generational change.*

And then go after it with all your passion!

Make today the day you choose to link arms with someone. To do life together.

To walk in wisdom as Jesus did.

THE *WISDOMWALKS* ROADMAP

WisdomWalks

Main Entry: wis·dom·walks

Pronunciation: ˈwizdəmˈwôks

Function: noun

Date: 2010

intentional, spiritual, life-changing connections.

Can you imagine what the disciples felt as they gradually realized they were walking with the God of the universe, the Creator of heaven and earth, the eventual Savior of the world? At first they had no idea who He really was, but His call compelled them to immediately leave everything they knew to follow Him. There was something special, something different, about Jesus. He could see things in people they couldn't see... do miraculous things they couldn't do. No wonder they were irresistibly drawn to Him.

Day after day they walked with Him along dirt roads, gathered together and ate meals, laughed and listened as they learned an entirely new way of doing life. Along the way their souls were satisfied because their longing for that "something more" was now gone. Jesus had what they wanted. He breathed life, purpose, passion, and power into an otherwise boring, unfulfilling life. The disciples tasted greatness. They touched eternity. And they would never be the same.

That's the same kind of power you'll experience as you become a WisdomWalker. Your time with Jesus will inspire you to walk in His footsteps, to hear His voice, to do what He did. You'll be challenged to love unconditionally, to live with integrity, to pray powerfully, and to do things greater than you've ever imagined! *WisdomWalks* will transform the way you think, feel, and the way you do life.

But this journey is not meant to be taken alone. It's not enough to walk with Jesus yourself. *WisdomWalks* is your opportunity to make a tremendous difference in the world—to share your experiences, your faith, and to influence others—by linking arms with another. It's a simple act, but powerfully life-changing.

Wisdom = skill at living.

It's applying truth, knowledge, discernment, and righteousness to every situation or decision.

The Power of Wisdom

Life is a series of forks in the road. Some directions and decisions are clearly right or wrong; others are merely multiple paths you could take. But all decisions take you down one of two paths. Proverbs 12:28 says the way of wisdom brings life immortal. (That's what I call a long-term investment!) Proverbs 14:12 says there is a path that seems right, but it ends up wrong.

That's why it's so important to be a WisdomWalker—someone who creates intentional, spiritual, life-changing connections. None of us can do life on our own. But very few of us have someone who taps us on the shoulder and says, "I see the potential for greatness in your life. Let's walk with Jesus together."

WisdomWalking is a lifelong process, not a program. A journey, not an encounter. You can't become who you need to be by remaining who you are.

*It all starts with **desire**.* Galatians 5:25 says, "Since we live by the Spirit, let us keep in step with the Spirit." Your life should reflect the fruit of the Spirit (verses 22–23), not the works of the flesh (verses 19–21). "Let us keep in step" means the desire to walk with Jesus every moment, and in every area of life, isn't a done deal; it's happening *right now.*

*It's fueled with **devotion**.* Walking as Jesus did is an all-or-nothing proposition. It's not about adding God into your life or sprinkling Him into your plans when you have time. When you say, "Whatever You want, God, not what I want," expect Him to take you up on that offer. Growth doesn't happen until you're outside your comfort zone.

*It's about setting your **direction**.* Just as coaches take athletes to a higher level of competition that they couldn't achieve on their own, our Master

Coach, Jesus Christ, has a game plan to take us from point A to point B. But there's a surprising flipside:

If you want to be blessed, bless others!
Want to be rich? Give it all away!
Want to be a friend? Then give up your life!
Want to be a leader? Then become a servant!

Jesus always wants us to advance to a new level—but it's rarely the one we expect.

If you don't change the direction you are going,
you're likely end up where you're heading.
JOHN C. MAXWELL

---

*It's a continuous journey to an ultimate **destination**.* When you're filled with God's wisdom, surrendered to His will, and you know your ultimate destination, you live a life worthy of Jesus, pleasing to Him in every way and bearing fruit in every good work (Colossians 1:9–14). You're patient; you give thanks always to God. You're so excited about what you're learning that you can't wait to pass the *WisdomWalks* experience on to others.

Live the Adventure!

WisdomWalking isn't as hard as you think. It's "walking alongside" another, and there are plenty of everyday opportunities to do so. Just take a look at all the ways *WisdomWalks* is already being used:

- to go deeper with a friend you meet one-on-one for coffee once a week
- to increase quality and quantity time with a child
- in a small group Bible study
- to get to know a student in your college dorm on a significant level
- to mentor a discouraged neighbor
- for the core teaching for men's accountability groups

- as a year-long Sunday school class
- for lively family dinners with intriguing discussions
- to mentor someone new in the Christian faith
- to help answer your coworker's questions about life
- to challenge a teen to walk like Jesus, talk like Jesus, and act like Jesus
- to start a once-a-week women's group

Come up with your own ideas too. Ask God to bring someone to mind—a friend, family member, employee, neighbor, or child. Ask that person if they would like to connect more deeply and intentionally with you and would be interested in a mentoring relationship. If that person agrees, these quick tips will help kick-off your adventure together:

- Decide when and where you'll meet, and how long you'll meet.
- Listen to each other's life concerns and questions.
- Think about each *WisdomWalks* entry—the principle, the questions, and the verses—before you meet.
- Write out your own thoughts about the subject of each chapter.
- Pray together at the beginning of every meeting to prepare your hearts and minds to focus on the life principle.

There are many ways to use the material, so be creative. Have one reader share the opening story aloud, or take turns reading. Journal your thoughts or discuss the *Be a WisdomWalker!* questions. Use the *Live It* section as quiet reflection and private prayer, or pray together for God to make His purposes known on this topic. *Maximize It* is perfect for "all-group" or one-on-one mentoring questions. To take your study deeper, look up the *Pass It On* Scriptures together, or use them for individual reflection during the week, then discuss your findings at your next meeting. Write the verse under *Be a WisdomWalker!* on one side of a notecard and the *WisdomWalks* principle on the other and post it on your bathroom mirror or the dashboard of your car. For additional study, dissect that verse or memorize it so you can ponder it later. Or why not create and share your own WisdomWalks from your unique life experiences? The possibilities for using WisdomWalks are endless. Just use your imagination!

Seven Steps to *WisdomWalks* Success

1. Engage God daily.

2. Pray for wisdom, discernment, and understanding.

3. Enjoy the journey.

4. Be authentic, honest, and transparent.

5. Value the relationships.

6. Be persistent and consistent.

7. Trust God for life-change.

DAN BRITTON AND JIMMY PAGE

As you walk through life with one another, remember that only *God* can bring about true heart change. Your role is to keep your eyes focused on Jesus and on the goal: to produce a WisdomWalker, who in turn will produce more WisdomWalkers. The fruit of an apple tree is not only apples but also another apple *tree*. And that's what *WisdomWalks* is all about: being a WisdomWalker and developing more WisdomWalkers. Don't miss out on this journey of a lifetime!

For additional study, read and reflect on:

- Exodus 3:15; 10:2; 12:26–27; 13:8, 14
- Deuteronomy 4:9, 6:5–9, 20–25; 6:5–9
- Judges 2:10
- Psalm 48:13; 70:13; 71:14–21; 78:1–12; 102:18
- 1 Corinthians 3:19
- 2 Timothy 2:2

40 LIFE PRINCIPLES
for a Significant & Meaningful Journey

1. Friends will make you or break you.

2. Be the person you want others to become.

3. What's in the well comes up in the bucket.

4. What you see is what you get.

5. Leave the mark of Jesus.

6. Your words are powerful and permanent.

7. A little humility goes a long way.

8. Put your money where your heart is.

9. Pay attention to God's little nudges.

10. God rewards good deeds done behind the scenes.

11. There is greatness in everyone.

12. Prayer *does* change things.

13. A step of faith often means "stay," not "go."

14. Guard yourself, because temptation lurks.

15. Give deeply of yourself, and you'll never go wrong.

16. Make your reputation match your reality.

17. Reclaim the real you.

18. Engage God daily—no matter what!

19. Little things always become big things.

20. Narrow the focus for greater life change.

21. Take every thought captive.

22. Forgive...then forgive again.

23. Expect it, get ready for it, and stand against it.

24. Put off the old; put on the new.

25. Be sold out for what you believe.

26. Life is a battleground, not a playground.

27. Follow the visions God places on your heart.

28. Life is not a "me" thing—it's a "we" thing.

29. Serve big, or go home!

30. Don't steal the glory.

31. Pray like your life depends on it.

32. God uses the few who are faith-full.

33. The path you pick leads to life or death.

34. Admit it, forget it, and get back in it.

35. Stay connected to the Source.

36. Do everything you can to change someone's world.

37. Make your life worth catching.

38. Live light and free on earth. Hold tight to heaven.

39. Be controlled by the Spirit, not your-self.

40. Live every day like it's your last.

DAN BRITTON serves as the Fellowship of Christian Athletes' Executive Vice President of Ministry Programs at the National Support Center in Kansas City. He has been on FCA staff since 1991, first serving for thirteen years in Virginia. Dan oversees the ministry advancement, including Camps, Coaches Ministry, Campus Ministry, Community Ministry, International Ministry, Inner-City Ministry, Sports-Specific Ministries, Training, and Resource Development. While at St. Stephens High School in Virginia and at the University of Delaware, Dan was a standout lacrosse player. He continued his career by playing professional indoor lacrosse for four years with the Baltimore Thunder, earning a spot on the All-Star team, and was nominated by his teammates for both the Service and Unsung Hero awards. Dan is now a frequent speaker at schools, churches, conferences, camps, conventions, and retreats. He still plays and coaches lacrosse and even enjoys running marathons. He is married to Dawn, whom he met in youth group in eighth grade, and they reside in Overland Park, Kansas, with their three children: Kallie, Abby and Elijah.

You can e-mail Dan at **dbritton@fca.org.**

Fellowship of Christian Athletes

Vision: To see the world impacted for Jesus Christ through the influence of athletes and coaches.

Mission: To present to athletes and coaches, and all whom they influence, the challenge and adventure of receiving Jesus Christ as Savior and Lord, serving Him in their relationships and in the fellowship of the church.

Values: Integrity • Serving • Teamwork • Excellence

About the Authors

JIMMY PAGE serves as a Vice President of Field Ministry and the National Director of the Health and Fitness ministry for the Fellowship of Christian Athletes. Growing up in the snow-country of Rochester New York, he became a three-sport athlete in high school and went on to graduate with two degrees from Virginia Tech. For nearly twenty years, he has been a leader in the medical fitness industry, operating wellness facilities affiliated with Sinai Hospital and Johns Hopkins. He currently hosts a daily radio segment and national podcast on iTunes called *Fit Life Today*, offering a blend of spiritual, mental, and physical health principles that promote abundant life. Jimmy is a frequent speaker and trainer for corporate and non-profit organizations, challenging people to transform their life, walk with Jesus, and influence others. He has a contagious enthusiasm and passion for life. As a lifelong athlete, Jimmy enjoys coaching, cycling, and triathlons. He is married to his college sweetheart, Ivelisse, and they reside in Maryland with their four children: Jimmy, Jacob, John, and Gracie.

You can e-mail Jimmy at **jpage@fca.org.**

Impacting the World for Christ through Sports

Fellowship of Christian Athletes is the world's largest sports ministry, reaching over two million people each year. Since 1954, FCA has cultivated Christian principles in local communities nationwide by encouraging, equipping, and empowering others to serve as examples and make a difference.

Fellowship of Christian Athletes | 8701 Leeds Road | Kansas City, MO 64129
www.fca.org • 800-289-0909